CHAPTER ONE

EDITOR'S
PICKS

The Horse Guards Inn

GU28 9AF | SEE P18 FOR MORE |

The Horse Guards Inn is located in the sleepy village of Tillington in the South Downs National Park, a few miles from Petworth. Filled with character, this 350-year-old pub is a great place to visit all year round. The vast, hidden garden is a picturesque haven of wildflowers and a great spot to catch the sun.

The Old Neptune

CT5 1EJ | SEE P17 FOR MORE |

The Old Neptune, known locally as Neppy, is a cosy, seaside boozer that is the subject of many a photo of Whitstable. The pub is located directly on the seafront which is an idyllic spot to spend an hour or two on a sunny afternoon.

The Sportsman

CT5 4BP | SEE P41 FOR MORE |

The Sportsman in Seasalter is an unlikely spot for a gastronomic delight but their reputation for fresh, quality fish is superb. The kitchen is run by Stephen Harris who has earned a Michelin star whilst cooking here. Stephen sources many quality ingredients from the local Monks Hill Farm.

The Noah's Ark

GU28 9ET | SEE P64 FOR MORE |

The Noah's Ark in Lurgashall is a bewitching 16th-century pub located just a stone's throw from Blackdown Hill on the borders of Surrey and West Sussex. Step inside to find a wonderful mix of old meets new - ancient fireplaces and low beams, alongside comfy leather sofas and contemporary design features.

The Mash Inn

HP14 4EB | SEE P66 FOR MORE |

The Mash Inn is a boutique Inn in Buckinghamshire with a prestigious reputation. Described as a restaurant with rooms, the open kitchen cooks the best seasonal ingredients on a bespoke wood-fired grill and many of the ingredients are sourced from the Inn's kitchen garden.

The Pandora Inn

TR11 5ST | SEE P95 FOR MORE |

Few pubs can claim to serve fish fresh from the boat, but Falmouth's 13th-century Pandora Inn does. But that's not the only thing that makes this inn special. Home to a cosy, character bar and restaurant, you can hunker down on a blustery day and enjoy food by the fire.

The Gurnard's Head

TR26 3DE | SEE P96 FOR MORE |

A landmark pub almost at the edge of England, the Gurnard's Head is your last stop for a pint and an open fire before the Atlantic Ocean. Between St Just and Zennor, this is genuine Cornwall. Wild, mysterious and beautiful, the Gurnard's Head is an inn that transports you back to when travel was that little bit slower.

The Port William

PL34 0HB | SEE P97 FOR MORE |

A cut above many Cornish inns, The Port William makes the most of its coastal location with floor-to-ceiling glazing in the restaurant, framing vast Atlantic views. Already a hotspot with surfers, you can enjoy a meal by the sea on a sunny day or cosy up and watch the lashing waves from a comfy spot beside the toasty wood burner.

The Inn at Welland

WR13 6LN | SEE P167 FOR MORE |

The Inn at Welland offers magnificent views over the Malvern Hills. This award-winning pub and restaurant is nationally renowned with a menu focusing on fresh local produce, made from 'scratch' by a team with a vision and passion for quality food.

The Lion Inn

GL54 5PS | SEE P127 FOR MORE |

Half an hour from Cheltenham, The Lion Inn in Winchcombe heralds a true Cotswolds retreat. The 15th-century coaching inn underwent a sympathetic renovation in 2011 and is now home to a rustic restaurant, cosy snug and comfortable bedrooms, with quirky character features.

The Ferry Inn

TQ8 8ET | SEE P159 FOR MORE |

Situated next to the harbour wall and overlooking the ombré blue water of picturesque Salcombe Harbour is The Ferry Inn. Owning one of the best positions in this beautiful region with its rolling hills and golden sands, the terrace, which sits parallel to the water, is one of the best spots for a drink in Salcombe.

The Ramsholt Arms

IP12 3AB | SEE P195 FOR MORE |

A popular riverside pub, situated on the scenic banks of the river Deben. The pub is located down a country lane and is a relaxing spot if you are looking to get away from the hustle and bustle. Dishes include favourites such as fish pie and slow cooked beef stew.

The Brisley Bell Inn

NR20 5DW | SEE P196 FOR MORE |

The Brisley Bell Inn is a 17th-century pub which has been tastefully and sympathetically renovated to become a stunning destination pub. In addition to the bar area, there is a quiet dining room and a cosy snug kitted out with books and an open fire.

The Gunton Arms

NR11 8TZ | SEE P197 FOR MORE |

The Gunton Arms is a unique pub located within a historic 1,000-acre deer park dating back to the 18th-century. Art dealer, Ivor Braka bought the pub in 2009 and spent 2 years renovating which included selecting appropriate pieces from his art collection with works by Tracey Emin and Damien Hirst now hung on the walls.

The Kings Head

NR25 7AR | SEE P198 FOR MORE |

The Kings Head in Letheringsett is nestled just outside the bustling Norfolk town of Holt. Housed within a handsome Georgian Manor from 1808 that has no less than three fires to create the bona fide country pub atmosphere. Ceilings are vaulted, shelves are adorned with books and grandfather clocks chime in the background.

The Drunken Duck

LA22 0NG | SEE P229 FOR MORE |

The Drunken Duck is located near Ambleside. Offering mesmerising views towards Windermere from its garden and terrace, the interior offers rustic country style with soft greens contrasting against chocolate leather armchairs, stripped oak floors and vintage artwork. With their own micro-brewery, the local ales and beers have a major appeal with locals and visitors.

The Cholmondeley Arms

SY14 8HN | SEE P230 FOR MORE |

In the heart of the Cheshire countryside, adjacent to Cholmondeley Castle and within a former Victorian village schoolhouse, is the Cholmondeley Arms. The pub has earned a reputation for its freshly cooked, locally sourced food from artisan bakers, farmers, butchers, fishermen and cheesemakers.

The Roebuck Inn

WA16 7HX | SEE P231 FOR MORE |

The Roebuck is an award-winning inn in the village of Mobberley dating back to 1708. The interior of rich burgundy banquettes, cabinets full of wine bottles and glasses, brass mirrors, dark woods and candlelight create a cosy ambience. The restaurant is more bistro than pub and the quirky decor gives the inn an air of eccentricity.

The Star Inn

YO62 5JE | SEE P263 FOR MORE |

Some six hundred years have made The Star Inn the charming pub that it is today. And what a pub, with food inspired by the inn's North York Moors location that has earned it a prestigious Michelin star. A title they have proudly held for four years in a row now.

The Lister Arms

BD23 4DB | SEE P264 FOR MORE |

The Lister Arms in Malham is a traditional coaching inn with captivating period features and an exterior embellished in vibrant green foliage. The inn's interior has been modernised whilst retaining its rich history and features, from its beams and wooden floors to its original fireplaces.

Craven Arms

BD23 6DA | SEE P265 FOR MORE |

The Craven Arms in Appletreewick is a picture-postcard, old English pub, with a great reputation for its food and real ale. The ale is all traditionally cask-conditioned and the artisan dishes are lovingly prepared from local ingredients on the premises.

Cook & Barker

NE65 9JY | SEE P266 FOR MORE |

A postcard of rural England, Newton-on-the-Moor's Cook & Barker Inn welcomes patrons with a charming stone façade, overflowing with flowers and country appeal. It's a rustic style that continues inside, with a distinctly luxurious touch. Think button-back seats, timber floorboards and exposed brick walls.

The Griffin Inn

TN22 3SS | SEE P13 FOR MORE |

Situated in the historic village of Fletching, The Griffin has been run by the Pullan family since 1979. During that time, The Griffin has built a considerable and national reputation for its food and wine. People come from far and wide to sample their cuisine and to absorb the views over the "Sussex Serengeti."

The Woolpack Inn

TN26 2LL | SEE P16 FOR MORE |

The Woolpack Inn is an exceptional pub in the depths of Kent offering top-notch pub grub, a friendly welcome as well as five beautiful and uniquely decorated rooms. Dishes include Fish Pie, Salt Marsh Beef Steak and Boozy Banana Split.

CHAPTER TWO

SOUTH
EAST

The Griffin Inn

TN22 3SS | **SUSSEX** | FLETCHING

Situated in the historic village of Fletching, The Griffin has been run by the Pullan family since 1979. During that time, The Griffin has built a considerable reputation for its food and wine. People come from far and wide to sample their cuisine.

The Griffin has a large, expertly landscaped garden with a stunning view over Sheffield Park. It includes a terrace area for al fresco dining, a large barbecue area and sloping lawns. 13 en-suite bedrooms are available.

ADDRESS

High Street, Fletching
TN22 3SS

PHONE

01825 722890

The Trout

SN7 8RF | OXFORDSHIRE | FARINGDON

Take to the Thames to reach this treasure chest of an Oxfordshire inn, perched on the riverbank at Tadpole Bridge, Faringdon. For the more conventional travellers, you can reach The Trout by road, too. The riverside theme makes a splash inside, with navy-toned accessories and suspended oars rubbing shoulders with the traditional building's stone fireplaces and timber beams.

From bar to bedrooms, this place has a sophisticated feel. The décor and furnishings are all on the luxe side of country, perfect for its Cotswolds setting. The pub's picturesque location is also the inspiration for its menu, which proudly purveys fish, game and all the country classics with a focus on fresh and local ingredients.

ADDRESS

Buckland Road, Faringdon
SN7 8RF

PHONE

01367 870382

The Stag Inn

GU28 9JP | SUSSEX | BALLS CROSS

A traditional country pub and boozer, The Stag Inn in Balls Cross welcomes visitors with its warm lighting, cosy interior and a roaring fire. Beams line the ceiling and walls are a mass of carriage brasses and picture frames - it's a nostalgic, friendly setting.

Just as you'd expect, hearty classics define the menu, while at the bar it's all about award-winning ales, including Badger's Fursty Ferret and Tangle Foot. Paying homage to its country setting on the edge of the South Downs National Park, The Stag Inn counts hounds and horses as visitors too.

ADDRESS
Kirdford Road, Balls Cross
GU28 9JP

PHONE
01403 820 241

The Woolpack Inn

TN26 2LL | KENT | WAREHORNE

The Woolpack Inn is an exceptional pub in the depths of Kent offering top-notch pub grub, a friendly welcome as well as five beautiful and uniquely decorated rooms. Dishes include Fish Pie, Salt Marsh Beef Steak and Boozy Banana Split.

The Woolpack Inn originated in the 16th-century inn and today well appointed and stylish rooms are available. Luxury is combined with quirkiness. Think brick walls, woodburners and sheepskin rugs juxtaposed against a vibrant colour palette and chandeliers. This inn exudes character and originality.

ADDRESS

Church Lane, Warehorne
TN26 2LL

PHONE

01233 732900

The Old Neptune

CT5 1EJ | **KENT** | WHITSTABLE

The Old Neptune, known locally as Neppy, is a cosy, seaside boozer and the subject of many a photo of Whitstable. The pub is located directly on the seafront which is an idyllic spot to spend an hour or two on a sunny afternoon. Its close position to the centre of the town makes it walkable from all of the popular eateries and boutiques.

They have a good selection of local ales and not so local lagers, as well as standard pub grub. The pebble beach on which it sits is family friendly and offers a relaxed environment. They host live music events and are also dog-friendly.

ADDRESS

Marine Terrace, Whitstable
CT5 1EJ

PHONE

01227 272262

The Horse Guards Inn

GU28 9AF | SUSSEX | TILLINGTON

The Horse Guards Inn is located in the sleepy village of Tillington in the South Downs National Park, a few miles from Petworth. Filled with character, this 350-year-old pub is a great place to visit all year round. The vast, hidden garden is a picturesque haven of wildflowers and a great spot to catch the sun.

The interior is relaxed and inviting with plenty of seating, oak beams and open log fires. Their food uses the very best in local produce with the menu changing daily and with the seasons. There are three en-suite "country-chic" bedrooms.

ADDRESS

Upperton Road, Tillington
GU28 9AF

PHONE

01798 342332

The Taverners

PO38 3HZ | ISLE OF WIGHT | GODSHILL

In the sleepy, quaint village of Godshill on the sunny Isle of White, The Taverners welcomes travellers and locals alike into its emporium of island food and booze. With a vegetable garden and fruit orchard on site, as well as a wealth of local producers who provide the best from land and sea, the menu at The Taverners is as local as it gets.

It's a story that continues at the bar, where you'll find the pub's own brew served alongside seasonal creations such as green walnut liqueur. The inn is a popular destination for visitors, who can also explore the pub's small store, which stocks artisan products made on the Isle of White. Inside, the pub is a cosy blend of timber beams, exposed brickwork and armchairs you'll sink into.

ADDRESS
High Street, Godshill
PO38 3HZ

PHONE
01983 840707

The Duke of Cumberland

GU27 3HQ | SUSSEX | FERNHURST

Nestling on the side of a steep hill in Henley near Fernhurst is the picturesque Duke of Cumberland Arms. It dates back to the 16th-century and benefits from breath-taking views and a delightful garden with ponds. Inside savour the old flagstones, rustic décor and local ales served straight from the barrel.

Roaring fires in every room create a warm and unbeatable atmosphere throughout the winter, while in the summer sitting in the evening sun enjoying views across the Sussex and Surrey countryside is magical. An exciting menu uses local produce; including vegetables from the pub's own allotment.

ADDRESS
Henley, Fernhurst
GU27 3HQ

PHONE
01428 652280

The Crown

TN34 3BN | SUSSEX | HASTINGS

The Crown is an independent pub in the old town of Hastings between East Hill country park and the beach. It offers a welcoming environment with friendly staff and plenty of local regulars. They serve Hastings brewed real ale and a delicious selection of home-cooked meals.

A relative newcomer to the Hastings scene, they have already built up a loyal following and reputation online. There are examples of local artists' work on the walls, daily newspapers and board games to play.

ADDRESS
64-66 All Saints' Street,
Hastings
TN34 3BN

PHONE
01424 465100

Aldeburgh, Suffolk

The Kings Head

TN25 5BN | KENT | WYE

The Kings Head is located in the historic village of Wye, at the foot of the Downs. They pride themselves on the quality of their food, service and environment. The pub's stylish interior is contemporary, with soft grey tones offset against chocolate leather banquette seating and pendent lighting.

In keeping with the countryside location, each of their guest rooms is simply and tastefully decorated. Reclaimed and vintage furniture is mixed with bright accents and modern accessories, to give the en-suite rooms a fresh and uncluttered feel. Breakfast is served in the restaurant.

ADDRESS

Church Street, Wye
TN25 5BN

PHONE

01233 812418

The Fox Goes Free

PO18 0HU | SUSSEX | CHARLTON

The Fox Goes Free is an alluring country pub in the quaint village of Charlton, West Sussex. The pub is 400 years old & full of oak beams, flint walls and open fireplaces. In warmer days, a pleasant afternoon can be spent in their large country garden overlooking the South Downs and nearby Goodwood Estate.

This listed building is surrounded by stunning, countryside walks. Wherever possible, their cuisine is locally sourced, home-made and includes favourites such as calamari and chorizo, fish pie and rib eye steak.

ADDRESS

Charlton Road, Charlton
PO18 0HU

PHONE

01243 811461

Sir Roger Tichborne

RH14 0QS | SUSSEX | BILLINGHURST

The Sir Roger Tichborne is a traditional country pub that celebrates locally sourced produce in charming surroundings. A large open fireplace, spacious open vaulted restaurant and other original features add character to this beautiful Victorian building, which overlooks delightful Sussex countryside.

The Sir Roger Tichborne is a quality destination pub for the whole family with its substantial beer garden, play area and child-friendly approach. They have a great reputation for their food and local ales. The menu changes with the seasons and popular pub classics such as the Tichburger and fish of the day are available year round.

ADDRESS

Loxwood Rd, Alfold Bars,
Billingshurst
RH14 0QS

PHONE

01403 751873

The Mermaid Inn

TN31 7EY | **SUSSEX** | **RYE**

The Mermaid Inn is situated in the beautiful medieval town of Rye, on a fantastic cobbled street full of history. The Inn has maintained the essence of true English charm for over 800 years and still has original features including a cellar dating back to 1156.

The whole inn boasts huge fireplaces, stories of smugglers, secret passageways and a huge list of famous visitors. Ghosts are rumoured to roam the pub and thirty-one bedrooms. Request a 'ghost-free' room when booking (if you prefer).

ADDRESS
Mermaid Street, Rye
TN31 7EY

PHONE
01797 223065

The Blacksmiths

PO20 7PR | SUSSEX | CHICHESTER

The Blacksmiths is an award-winning pub in Donnington near Chichester. With its cosy wood fires, an extensive garden and fine cuisine, a passion for local food is at the heart of every plate. The kitchen team also use high-quality ingredients from their own garden and farm.

At The Blacksmiths you can make a night of it as they have three furnished en-suite rooms, full of homely comforts. Music and movie nights are often held at the pub, so make sure you don't miss out.

ADDRESS
Selsey Rd, Donnington, Chichester
PO20 7PR

PHONE
01243 785578

The Pointer

HP18 9RT | BUCKINGHAMSHIRE | BRILL

The Pointer in Brill is a red brick beauty in Buckinghamshire, ploughed forwards by a commitment to local produce and sustainable methods. The 16th-century bar was renovated in 2012 and now offers a welcoming array of wingback armchairs, plush sofas and character furniture to relax into. Try the Pointer Pint at the bar, among a selection of local ales, as well as wine made from grapes grown less than 10 miles away.

Quality ingredients are at the top of the menu, with meat and charcuterie produced from the pub's own 250-acre farm. It's an exciting opportunity to taste the native meat, including Longhorn cattle and Hampshire Down sheep. The team also tend to a kitchen garden and bake their own bread – farm to fork dining done properly.

ADDRESS
27 Church St, Brill
HP18 9RT

PHONE
01844 238339

The Gloucester Old Spot

GL51 9SY | GLOUCESTERSHIRE | CHELTENHAM

A testament to their commitment to serve the local village and neighbouring towns well, The Gloucester Old Spot is among the rare breed of pubs to serve food seven days a week. The bar is cosy and rustic and the restaurant a real treat. Enjoy seasonal and locally sourced food from comfy country furniture, while the flickering log burner and atmospheric lighting give the exposed brick walls a sense of theatre.

Local ciders and hand-pulled ales keep the bar well supported, with drinks changing frequently. The historic towns of Tewkesbury and Cheltenham are also conveniently located nearby.

ADDRESS

Tewkesbury Rd, Piffs Elm, Cheltenham
GL51 9SY

PHONE

01242 680321

The Yew Tree

RG20 9SE | **HAMPSHIRE** | HIGHCLERE

With interiors that feel like a contemporary hunting lodge, this stylish Hampshire pub has become somewhat of a destination thanks to its AA Rosette-winning menu and proximity to Highclere Castle.

The Yew Tree dates back to the 17th century and, as such, offers an enchanting blend of old and new. A contemporary copper bar reflects the glow of the old fireplaces – an inviting place to pop into for a pint. For sunnier days, there's also an alfresco bar in the garden. Locally caught fish and game take centre stage on the menu and there are eight cosy bedrooms featuring William Morris wallpaper to tempt you.

ADDRESS

Hollington Cross andover Rd,
Highclere
RG20 9SE

PHONE

01635 253360

PLACES WE LOVE

Mermaid Street, Rye

The Cat Inn

RH19 4PP | SUSSEX | WEST HOATHLY

The Cat Inn, West Hoathly, is a 16th-century free house with four bedrooms. The village is a haven for walkers, ideally placed on the Western edge of the Ashdown Forest and the surrounding area is blessed with a plethora of attractive places to visit.

Local breweries including Harvey's of Lewes, provide refreshment alongside still and sparkling wines from the local area. Food is seasonal and of a high quality.

ADDRESS

North Lane, West Hoathly
RH19 4PP

PHONE

01342 810369

The Mayflower

SO41 3QD | **HAMPSHIRE** | **LYMINGTON**

The Mayflower is located in the pretty Georgian Market town of Lymington with its cobbled streets and seaside walks. The theme of this pub is very much nautical with coastal tones and sailing paraphernalia that adorn the walls to satisfy the clientele from the nearby marina. Parquet floors, leather armchairs and open log fires all add to the ambience.

Food is seasonal and local with dishes including Lymington seafood pappardelle and slow roast pork belly. They have a number of comfortable rooms to stay overnight and serve breakfast to all from 8am. Well behaved dogs are welcome.

ADDRESS

King's Saltern Road, Lymington
SO41 3QD

PHONE

01590 672160

The Coach and Horses

RH17 7JF | SUSSEX | HAYWARDS HEATH

If you are one for good food in a traditional country setting then the Coach and Horses in Danehill is sure to fulfil your expectations. Situated on the edge of the Ashdown Forest and hidden down a country lane, the location is peaceful and rural and from the large garden, you'll enjoy views of the Sussex Downs.

Since 1847, the Coach and Horses has been winning awards for their beer selection and locally sourced produce. Popular dishes include haddock soufflé, chargrilled cauliflower and Thai red mussel curry.

ADDRESS

School Lane, Haywards Heath
RH17 7JF

PHONE

01825 740369

The Bull

BN6 8TA | **SUSSEX** | DITCHLING

The Bull in Ditchling is one of the oldest buildings in Ditchling village and has been welcoming travellers and locals for over 500 years. Located inside the South Downs National Park, yet the Bull is only 15 minutes from Brighton and the sea.

Low timber beams, open fires and deep leather sofas make for a cosy retreat on chillier days while in the summer there's a terrace to enjoy and a large garden with a play area and views of the Downs. Food is served at the bar and in the garden and there are four en-suite rooms found hidden through a secret door.

ADDRESS
2 High Street, Ditchling,
Brighton
BN6 8TA

PHONE
01273 843147

Fisherman's Cottage

PO37 6BN | ISLE OF WIGHT | SHANKLIN

If you fancy food by the sea, the Isle of White's Fisherman's Cottage will tick all your boxes with its seafront location and thatched pub charm. You'll count boats and breakers for neighbours as you enjoy a pint at Shanklin's oldest pub, built in 1817. It's located close to Shanklin Chine, a breath-taking gorge that is an island must-see.

The water also inspires the menu, with seasonal fish, Bembridge crab and lobster and an epic fish and chips taking pride of place alongside traditional meat dishes. Catch the sun on the patio or hunker down in the dining room – this pub is a gem whatever the weather.

ADDRESS

Shanklin Esplanade, Shanklin,
Isle of White
PO37 6BN

PHONE

01983 863882

The Chimney House

BN1 5DF | SUSSEX | BRIGHTON

The Chimney House is a traditional pub in the heart of Brighton next to the Seven Dials. Ingredients are sourced from within Sussex with fish from Shoreham and Newhaven, fruit and vegetables from local farms and glasshouses and meat from Garlic Wood Farm.

The environment is relaxed and family friendly and the food is honest and unpretentious. Their Sunday Roast is popular with locals and visitors alike, this pub has an exceptional reputation.

ADDRESS

28 Upper Hamilton Road,
Brighton
BN1 5DF

PHONE

01273 556708

The Greyhound

SO20 6EY | HAMPSHIRE | STOCKBRIDGE

The Greyhound on the Test is an award-winning pub that serves delicious food & drink in Stockbridge. This establishment goes above and beyond with quality service and excellent produce.

The kitchen uses the best of local and seasonal produce under the direction of Chris Heather and the log burning fire during the cooler months is a characterful addition. The rooms are the height of country-lux and a beautiful contrast against the original features from this 16th-century inn.

ADDRESS

31 High Street, Stockbridge
SO20 6EY

PHONE

01264 810833

The Sportsman

CT5 4BP | KENT | WHITSTABLE

The Sportsman in Seasalter is an unlikely spot for a gastronomic delight but their reputation for fresh, quality fish is superb. The kitchen is run by Stephen Harris who has earned a Michelin star whilst cooking here. Stephen sources many quality ingredients from the local Monks Hill Farm.

The atmosphere is relaxed with well-worn decor throughout, the energy here is focused entirely on the food they serve. The tasting menu is legendary, allow 3+ hours to work through the 10 courses. If you are a foodie then The Sportsman should be high up on your bucket list.

ADDRESS

Faversham Road, Whitstable
CT5 4BP

PHONE

01227 273370

The Poet

TN12 7JH | KENT | TONBRIDGE

The Poet in Matfield has recently benefited from a complete renovation. The restaurant sits within a 17th Century building named after war poet Siegfried Sassoon, who was born and raised in Matfield.

The kitchen is run by South African chef, Petrus Madutlela who focuses on the three pillars of quality, locality and seasonality. Dishes include 28 day-aged rib eye with shallots, tuna tataki & blood orange sorbet. Non-delinquent dogs are welcome.

ADDRESS

Maidstone Road, Matfield, Tonbridge
TN12 7JH

PHONE

01892 722416

The Bell Inn

TN5 7AS | SUSSEX | TICEHURST

The Bell Inn offers a truly local experience whilst warmly welcoming guests from all over the country. The provenance of the food is key to their ingredient selection and the menu features the best of Sussex's local fish, meat and dairy.

Proudly showcasing the suppliers of their cuisine, the pub has become renowned for its food and ambience. Stylish, eccentric and rustic, The Bell Inn offers an authentic pub experience from the moment you arrive. Built around 1296, this is an historic pub with an excellent and well-deserved reputation.

ADDRESS

High Street, Ticehurst
TN5 7AS

PHONE

01580 200300

The Queen's Inn

TN18 4EY | KENT | HAWKHURST

This immaculately restored inn provides a luxurious country retreat to eat, drink and indulge. The Queen's Inn can be found in the scenic town of Cranbrook. Fresh, locally sourced ingredients are expertly combined and served in their stylish, yet welcoming surroundings.

They offer an extensive handpicked wine list, a range of local beer, ale and cider, all served next to their roaring log fire. Guest rooms are available and have been elegantly designed and finished, with each individually styled to create its own personality and story.

ADDRESS

Rye Road, Hawkhurst
TN18 4EY

PHONE

01580 754233

The Three Chimneys

TN27 8LW | **KENT** | **BIDDENDEN**

The Three Chimneys is an award-winning, independent country pub in Biddenden. The building dates back to 1420. Dark oak beams, a roaring fire and five separate dining areas make this a characterful and relaxed venue for a pint or a bite to eat.

Craig Smith, who packed in his City job to take over the pub in 1999 serves Welsh Rarebit, Haddock Fishcakes and deep fried brie. There are five luxury bedrooms available but oddly, only two chimneys. An ideal refreshment stop-off if you are visiting Sissinghurst Castle or Scotney Castle. Dogs are welcome.

ADDRESS
Hareplain Road, Biddenden
TN27 8LW

PHONE
01580 291472

PLACES WE LOVE
St Ives, Cornwall

The Barrow House

TN27 9DJ | **KENT** | **EGERTON**

A much-loved village pub with a stylish overhaul. The Barrow House was crafted in 1576 using timbers from sailing ships. The pub serves its local community well, providing good seasonal food and a relaxing place to unwind. Their handcrafted burgers are made in house and their bread is baked daily.

Idyllic in its countryside location, enjoy real ale and filling yet refined fare. The decor is immaculate, merging modern style with country accents. For those who want to spend more time in the village or explore the local area, there are three beautiful bedrooms upstairs.

ADDRESS

The Street, Egerton, Faversham
TN27 9DJ

PHONE

01233 756599

The Duke William

CT3 1QP | KENT | ICKHAM

Situated just ten minutes outside of the historic City of Canterbury, The Duke William is a contemporary and stylish pub. With a roaring fire during the winter months, the idyllic garden is full of hanging baskets, potted plants, an olive tree and herb boxes during the summer.

The menu is built around the best local produce and suppliers the surrounding countryside and coastline have to offer. Seasonality is key, which is why their menus are constantly evolving. Guest rooms are softly decorated in Farrow and Ball shades, with vibrant pops of colour on contemporary furnishings.

ADDRESS

The Street, Ickham, Sheerness
CT3 1QP

PHONE

01227 721308

The Plough Inn

RH5 6HD | SURREY | DORKING

The Plough Inn in Dorking focuses on the seasonal availability of local food, from the freshest fruit and vegetables to the grass-fed beef. They only use the best ingredients, sourced from many small, award-winning suppliers in the area. Locally produced vintages, small batch gins and single malts also appear on the menu.

The pub even has its own Leith Hill microbrewery on-site. Established in 1996, the brewery uses traditional methods and 100% natural ingredients. Six individually styled contemporary bedrooms are available with ensuite facilities.

ADDRESS

Abinger Road, Coldharbour
RH5 6HD

PHONE

01306 711793

The Duke of Cambridge

GU10 2DD | **SURREY** | **FARNHAM**

Dedicated to sourcing from British farmers and producers and using only sustainable ingredients, The Duke of Cambridge focuses on using produce which has travelled very few miles from the farm to the fork. The Tilford Brewery is located next door to the pub and provides award-winning ales.

This modern pub is a hit with dog walkers and families alike thanks to its beautiful positioning within the Surrey countryside and its custom-built adventure play area. The garden grill and bar, open during the summer months, is a popular spot to enjoy al fresco dining.

ADDRESS
Tilford Road, Farnham
GU10 2DD

PHONE
01252 792236

The Abinger Hatch

RH5 6HZ | **SURREY** | DORKING

The Abinger Hatch is a traditional family-owned English pub with foliage creeping over the doorways and windows. With roaring wood-burners keeping the pub cosy on colder days, dogs and kids are warmly welcomed. The menu offers homemade classic British pub fare and Sunday roasts are popular.

The 18th century Abinger Hatch is situated in the charming hamlet of Abinger Common and is undergoing some refurbishment this year to improve the interior and to restore some of its original features under the new ownership.

ADDRESS

Abinger Ln, Abinger Common
RH5 6HZ

PHONE

01306 730737

The Merry Harriers

GU8 4DR | SURREY | GODALMING

In the scenic village of Hambledon in the Surrey Hills Area of Outstanding Natural Beauty, The Merry Harriers dates back to the 16th century. This traditional village pub has a truly local feel, with crackling fires and a menu using often foraged ingredients and where possible, locally sourced within a 15-mile radius.

The resident llamas living behind the Inn, add character and fun for all ages. Seven contemporary en-suite bedrooms are furnished to a high standard with rustic charm and featuring the pub's ancient oak beams.

ADDRESS
Hambledon Road, Godalming
GU8 4DR

PHONE
01428 682883

The Stag on the River

GU7 2QG | **SURREY** | **GODALMING**

The charming Surrey village of Lower Eashing is home to 15th-century The Stag on the River, an attractive red-brick pub beside the River Wey. A sociable beer garden invites you to soak up the sun in summer while the river burbles by. Inside, heritage-style wallpapers, tweed soft furnishings and an open fire offer a comfortable, country experience with a touch of luxury.

In the kitchen, ingredients are kept as local as possible with sustainability key. Local flavours also inject personality into the bar menu, with Hog's Back Brewery Hazy Hog and Hogstar lagers a highlight. After a day out in Godalming or Guildford, The Stag on the River's seven indulgent bedrooms promise an idyllic country retreat.

ADDRESS

Lower Eashing, Godalming
GU7 2QG

PHONE

01483 421568

The Anchor Inn

GU34 4NA | HAMPSHIRE | ALTON

Conveniently located close to the A31 between Winchester and Guildford, the Anchor Inn has long been a favourite for the local village and tourists alike. Packed to the rafters with history, enjoy a local ale beside the traditional bar and open fire, or take a seat in the atmospheric restaurant, which serves elegant, seasonal fare and award-winning wines.

Set in the Hampshire countryside, this country inn keeps its surroundings close to its heart. The menu showcases the best of British ingredients in beautifully presented dishes, with a garden looking onto fields that offers dining with a view. Upstairs, you'll find comfortable, country bedrooms with antique furniture, named after writers and each with its own collection of tomes.

ADDRESS
Lower Froyle, Alton, Fording-bridge
GU34 4NA

PHONE
01420 23261

The Kingham Plough

OX7 6YD | OXFORDSHIRE | KINGHAM

Arguably one of the best-loved pubs in the Cotswolds, the award-winning Kingham Plough is only 10 minutes from the sought-after town of Chipping Norton. Offering a unique balance between high-quality dining and family-friendly experiences, all in a charming, honey-stone setting, the pub has become a destination worth visiting in its own right.

Provenance is the centre from which everything radiates. From the locally sourced hedgerow liqueurs to the fresh ingredients, delivered daily, the menu is modern, memorable and an authentic taste of Oxfordshire. And with the Cotswolds countryside on the doorstep, a stay in the six classically decorated bedrooms in shades of cream, pink and duck egg blue is the perfect after dinner treat.

ADDRESS
The Green, Kingham
OX7 6YD

PHONE
01608 658327

The Kings Head

OX7 6XQ | **OXFORDSHIRE** | BLEDINGTON

In a prime position on the village green, The Kings Head in Bledington is a true country idyll. The cosy bar has built a reputation for its selection of locally brewed lagers and ales, with an inglenook stone fireplace to drink them next to. The restaurant purveys hearty dishes with a refined twist however on a sunny day, there's no better place to be than the garden, with views onto the burbling stream just a stone's throw away.

Since opening in 2000, the owners have curated a team of quality, local suppliers to ensure the best ingredients feature on each plate. Six miles from Chipping Norton, this pub makes a brilliant base from which to explore the Cotswolds, with a choice of bedrooms above the inn or in the charming courtyard.

ADDRESS

The Green, Bledington
OX7 6XQ

PHONE

01608 658365

Killingworth Castle

OX20 1EJ | OXFORDSHIRE | WOOTTON

Having first opened its doors to the local people of Wootton in 1637, Killingworth Castle has built an impressive clientele, including Sir Winston Churchill in days gone by. The current custodians took to the helm in 2012, forging an award-winning future for the pub with such a prestigious past. The ambience is welcoming and full of charm.

The hearty menu makes the most of British pub classics, served with flair and finesse in a friendly setting befitting the pub's rural location. Local produce guides the menu, while the owners' very own Cotswolds-brewed craft beer range adds interest at the bar. With Blenheim Palace on the doorstep, the inn's eight luxurious bedrooms welcome you to extend your stay and explore.

ADDRESS

Glympton Road, Wootton, Burford
OX20 1EJ

PHONE

01993 811401

Mr Hanbury's Mason Arms

OX29 6XN | **OXFORDSHIRE** | SOUTH LEIGH

A thatched Oxfordshire pub with plenty of curb appeal, the interior of this inn is just as charming as it is outside. Chunky wooden furniture, eye-catching wallpaper and eclectic soft furnishings give the space a unique identity. It is a comfortable, memorable and relaxing place in which to enjoy a meal with friends.

The menu takes simple, seasonal ingredients and combines them in creative ways, with a choice of traditional English dishes to enjoy beside the roaring fire. There's also a carefully curated selection of wines, the opportunity to try local ales and country cocktails to quaff too. There are five bedrooms and two suites for those who'd like to stay the night.

ADDRESS

Station Road, South Leigh
OX29 6XN

PHONE

01993 656238

The Nut Tree Inn

OX5 2RE | OXFORDSHIRE | MURCOTT

The Nut Tree Inn is an enchanting thatched pub with modern, Michelin-starred menu, four miles from the bustling Oxfordshire town of Bicester. The gardens are filled with blossoming hanging baskets and attractive plants, creating a country welcome that appeals to locals and visitors alike.

Steeped in over 500 years of history, the bar is comfortably clad with plush cushions, leather sofas and exposed stone walls – an attractive, beautifully preserved setting in which to enjoy a pint or glass of gin beside the fire. Dinner is served in the same cosy surrounds, but there's also a light and airy, but no less atmospheric, dining room for a more formal experience. Freshly baked bread, quality suppliers and a dynamic menu are The Nut Tree Inn's ingredients for success.

ADDRESS
Main Street, Murcott, Oxon
OX5 2RE

PHONE
01865 331253

The Five Alls

GL7 3JQ | **GLOUCESTERSHIRE** | FILKINS

Tucked in the quaint Cotswolds village of Filkins, The Five Alls offers an exciting blend of traditional English fare with an Italian twist. The honey-stone inn covered in climbing plants exudes country appeal – this is a theme that continues inside, with logs piled high, charming flagstone floors and a cosy fireplace to gather around.

Seasonal cocktails, The Five Alls' house ale and an extensive wine list offer a tipple for every taste, while a menu influenced by the town's artisan producers promises a foodie treat, combined with the head chef's Italian connections. Upstairs, there are four en-suite rooms above the inn and a further five bespoke bedrooms reached from the picturesque garden.

ADDRESS
Filkins, Lechlade
GL7 3JQ

PHONE
01367 860875

PLACES WE LOVE

Staithes, Yorkshire

The Noah's Ark

GU28 9ET | SUSSEX | LURGASHALL

The Noah's Ark in Lurgashall is a bewitching 16th-century pub located just a stone's throw from Blackdown Hill on the borders of Surrey and West Sussex. Step inside to find a wonderful mix of old meets new - ancient fireplaces and low beams, alongside comfy leather sofas and contemporary design features.

This child-friendly pub is renowned for its seasonal food and great service. The front garden of the Noah's Ark overlooks the large village green making it a wonderful place to sit during the summer months and watch the locals play cricket.

ADDRESS

The Green, Lurgashall
GU28 9ET

PHONE

01428 707346

The Dog at Wingham

CT3 1BB | KENT | WINGHAM

Located 20 minutes' drive from the historic city of Canterbury is the up-and-coming The Dog at Wingham. At its heart are trusted, local suppliers. Even the bread is baked in the same village. The menu is fresh, authentic and offers a taste of the seasons. With plenty of local ales, over 40 types of gin and a wonderful selection of wines from vineyards near and far, the bar is stocked with something for everyone too.

Upstairs are eight elegantly furnished bedrooms. Each has its own identity, including an impressive four-poster room and they are united by the luxury and comfort they offer to guests. A charming base for a visit to the 'Garden of England'.

ADDRESS
Canterbury Road,
Wingham,
Canterbury
CT3 1BB

PHONE
01227 720339

The Mash Inn

HP14 4EB | BUCKINGHAMSHIRE | RADNAGE

The Mash Inn is a boutique Inn in Buckinghamshire with a prestigious reputation. Described as a restaurant with rooms, the open kitchen cooks the best seasonal ingredients on a bespoke wood-fired grill and many of the ingredients are sourced from the Inn's kitchen garden. The founder Nick Mash believes in the authentic country dining experience and in supporting local craftsmen and producers.

Foraging for ingredients, pulling vegetables out of the ground and having them on your plate within a couple of hours, only reinforces this unique and yet traditional approach to country dining. The Inn is not suitable for under 16s. Rooms are rustic and luxurious and offer beautiful countryside views.

ADDRESS

Horseshoe Rd, Radnage
HP14 4EB

PHONE

01494 482440

Sir Charles Napier

OX39 4BX | OXFORDSHIRE | OXON

The beautiful, 18th-century flint embellished Sir Charles Napier Inn sits in a beautiful spot in the Chilterns amongst scenic English gardens. With two roaring wood fires crackling away, the food here is exceptional and the views are mesmerising. The Inn has earned its reputable status over the decades it has been established.

The Sunday roasts here are legendary and ingredients are based on their seasonal availability. Inside, the atmosphere is cosy and leans towards formal in the dining area, which is carpeted and resembles a country house dining room. People travel from far and wide to experience Sir Charles Napier Inn and have done for years.

ADDRESS

Spriggs Alley, Chinnor, Oxon
OX39 4BX

PHONE

01494 483011

The Beehive

SL6 3SH | BERKSHIRE | WHITE WALTHAM

Set in the Berkshire countryside and overlooking the village cricket ground is The Beehive. Chef Patron Dominic Chapman is a Michelin-starred laureate with an aim to "offer beautiful food in a real English pub." With a reputation for its excellent seasonal menu, dishes represent Britain and its abundant produce.

The interior is light and contemporary with quirky details and artwork. The dining room has mismatched wood tables and lots of natural light. In the cooler months, the open fire is a cosy addition. Chapman's objective is to create delicious dishes utilising Great Britain's wonderful produce.

ADDRESS

Waltham Road, White Waltham
SL6 3SH

PHONE

01628 822877

The Kings Head

SO21 2JW | **HAMPSHIRE** | WINCHESTER

The King's Head stands on the edge of the New Forest in the village of Hursley, where a coaching inn first opened in 1810. The popular city of Winchester and its famed medieval cathedral are around five miles away. Old meets new inside the restaurant, with grey painted shutters and chunky wooden tables adding a contemporary rustic twist to the Georgian building's high ceilings and period features.

Food is locally sourced and foraged, with many ingredients coming from the surrounding Hampshire countryside, to create a diverse menu that is complemented by fine wines. The inn also features a traditional skittles alley and eight striking bedrooms, each named after residents of the nearby Hursley Estate. Dogs are welcome patrons, too

ADDRESS

Main Road, Hurlsey, Winchester
SO21 2JW

PHONE

01962 775208

The Swan

GU8 4TY | SURREY | CHIDDINGFOLD

Set on the edge of the picturesque Surrey countryside, The Swan Inn at Chiddingfold is a relaxed contemporary pub with a focus on serving delicious food and quality drinks in a warm, welcoming atmosphere. The Swan Inn derives its name from the swans elegantly gliding on the village pond and nearby river.

This is an AA four star inn with an award-winning restaurant menu. The pub garden is glorious on summer days. Open fires, stained glass, fresh flowers and comfy banquettes make this the perfect pub environment. The menu is dictated to by the seasons and the very best produce available.

ADDRESS

Petworth Road, Chiddingfold
GU8 4TY

PHONE

01428 684688

The Three Lions

SP6 2HF | **HAMPSHIRE** | FORDINGBRIDGE

The cosy feel and charming beams come as pleasant surprise when you step inside The Three Lions in Fordingbridge, Hampshire. Headed up by former Michelin-starred chef Mike and Jayne, this pub presents classic cuisine in a comfortable setting in the New Forest National Park.

Take a seat in the dining room and choose from over 100 carefully chosen wines to accompany your meal. A similar attention to detail is paid to the dishes, making the most of local ingredients. There's a traditional wooden bar to chat beside and a crackling log fire to gather around, ensuring a relaxed experience.

ADDRESS
Stuckton, Nr. Fordingbridge
SP6 2HF

PHONE
01425 652489

Gomshall Mill

GU5 9LB | SURREY | GUILDFORD

Situated on the River Tillingbourne, Gomshall Mill is beautiful timber-framed mill dating from Medieval times. Ancient floorboards, oak beams and open fires create an authentic and traditional pub environment.

British classics feature on the menu with some international fusion influences. The mill existed at the time of the Domesday book. The existing building from the 1600's still contains some of the original milling machinery.

ADDRESS
Gomshall, Guildford
GU5 9LB

PHONE
01483 203 060

The Plough Inn

ME13 0HY | KENT | FAVERSHAM

Serving up daily specials, Sunday roasts and pub classics, The Plough Inn is a tempting retreat defined by Kentish food and drink. Located in the North Downs, the pub is independently owned and family-run and sits within a picturesque garden. With rolling countryside on the doorstep, it's the perfect place to relax and refuel after a bracing country walk.

The Plough is making its mark as a boozer too, with 13 rums, 20 gins and an array of Kentish ciders, lagers and white wines from vineyards including Chapel Down. Newly renovated bedrooms will soon be available for guests, while camping and five motorhome pitches in the grounds already invite you to eat, drink and be merry, then stay the night.

ADDRESS

Stalisfield Road, Faversham
ME13 0HY

PHONE

01795 890 256

PLACES WE LOVE

Whitby, Yorkshire

The Angel Inn

GU28 0BG | SUSSEX | PETWORTH

Idyllically based in the South Downs National Park, The Angel Inn, has medieval origins and is situated just 300 yards from the Market Square, the centre of Petworth, one of Britain's most attractive market towns. The menu serves excellent food made with fresh and seasonal ingredients.

The beautiful interior and bar boast ships beams, wooden and slate floors, stone walls and three fireplaces, one of which is used to spit roast joints of meat. There are six comfortable bedrooms, all with an en-suite and decorated with a country-luxe aesthetic.

ADDRESS

1 Angel St, Petworth
GU28 0BG

PHONE

01798 344445

The Blackboys Inn

TN22 5LG | **SUSSEX** | **UCKFIELD**

Nestled into a quiet lane in an idyllic East Sussex village, The Blackboys Inn epitomises old-world English charm with its flower-filled garden and picturesque weather-boarded exterior. Hops hang from the rafters, brasses decorate the beams and brick walls glow in the hazy light. This 14th-century pub has atmosphere on tap – especially if you visit on one of their popular open mic or quiz nights.

Meals are hearty with a homely touch and Five Harveys Ale keeps the bar full. If you'd like to make a weekend of it, there are five comfortable bedrooms too.

ADDRESS
Lewes Rd, Blackboys, Uckfield
TN22 5LG

PHONE
01825 890283

The Earl of March

PO18 0BQ | SUSSEX | CHICHESTER

This early 18th Century pub is set against the backdrop of the South Downs and the Goodwood Estate in the village of Lavant. This is reportedly the location where William Blake, the famous poet and composer wrote the words to Jerusalem in 1803.

Giles Thompson, the former Executive Head Chef of The Ritz in London took the pub over in 2007. The food here has a fantastic reputation and Thompson's use of the finest produce, often from organic sources, creates truly exceptional dishes. The pub has a 'contemporary country' aesthetic and beautiful views from the garden over the rolling countryside.

ADDRESS
Lavant Rd, Chichester
PO18 0BQ

PHONE
01243 533993

The Anchor Bleu

PO18 8LS | **SUSSEX** | **BOSHAM**

Situated in the picturesque harbourside village of Bosham, The Anchor Bleu is steeped in history and remains an exceptionally popular location for decent food and scenic drinks overlooking the harbour. The views over the water are mesmerising on a sunny day.

With its proximity to the water, seafood features highly on the menu and the drinks menu carries an extensive range of wines and cask ales. Inside the pub is light and contemporary in style with original features and eclectic furnishings.

ADDRESS

High St, Bosham, Chichester
PO18 8LS

PHONE

01243 573956

The Globe

TN31 7NX | SUSSEX | RYE

The Globe Inn is a cosy neighbourhood pub with a national reputation. The menus reflect the region's access to the sea and salt marshes. The abundance of fresh local ingredients from humane, traceable farms are incorporated into the delicious dishes.

Roaring fires, candlelight and quirky accessories create a vibrant and intimate environment at The Globe Inn. The pub also carries a fantastic collection of local ales, craft beers and artisan gins alongside classic favourites.

ADDRESS
10 Military Rd, Rye
TN31 7NX

PHONE
01797 225220

Farmer Butcher Chef

TN31 7NX | SUSSEX | CHICHESTER

Situated on the magnificent and historic Goodwood Estate, Farmer Butcher Chef is renowned for its exceptional menu and creative approach to sustainability, with its produce sourced from the estate's very own Home Farm. The restaurant has a distinctive and pioneering approach to farm-to-table cuisine with an emphasis on flavour, quality and provenance.

Their innovative and passionate chef Darron Bunn has won two Michelin stars and is passionate about bringing nostalgic cooking back to life in all of his dishes. The restaurant exudes English country style with a roaring fire and eccentric English paraphernalia.

ADDRESS

Goodwood, New Barn Hill,
Chichester
PO18 0QB

PHONE

01243 755070

The Hinds Head

SL6 2AB | |

Established as a hunting lodge and coaching inn in the 1400s, The Hind's Head in Bray is a traditional pub by Heston Blumenthal, infused with the innovative and creative ethos he applies to food and for which he is renowned. The menu reflects the establishment's British heritage.

With an interior of soft blues, stained glass and oxblood leather banquettes set against original beams, dark wood flooring and inglenook fireplaces, this Michelin-starred restaurant offers astounding culinary genius in the relaxed setting of a traditional pub environment in one of the most idyllic riverside village locations of Bray.

ADDRESS

High Street, Bray, Berkshire
SL6 2AB

PHONE

01628 626 151

The Lewes Arms

BN7 1YH | SUSSEX | LEWES

The Lewes Arms is over 200 years old and one of Lewes' favourite traditional pubs. Positioned close to the town's beautiful Norman Castle, this is an authentic pub experience with a rustic interior and down-to-earth atmosphere.

In the evenings, candles light the pub and patrons try to grab the limited seating by the open fire. This is an unpretentious pub and Sunday roasts are popularly served with the local Harvey's ale. Evenings are lively as the pub is small and popular.

ADDRESS

Mount Place, Lewes, East Sussex
BN7 1YH

PHONE

01273 473152

The Anchor

GU23 6AE | SURREY | RIPLEY

The Anchor in Ripley is one of Surrey's oldest and most historic pubs with a reputation for its flavoursome food using local and regional produce. Parts of the pub date back to the early 16th century when the pub was originally built as an almshouse but today the tasteful and stylish interior has more of a contemporary appeal.

Mike Wall-Palmer has a passion for quality, locally produced ingredients and incorporates these into his dishes. He also runs seasonal Supper Club evenings which are popular with locals and visitors alike. The courtyard offers a lovely al fresco spot during the warmer months.

ADDRESS
High Street, Ripley
GU23 6AE

PHONE
01483 211866

The Milk House

TN17 2JG | **KENT** | SISSINGHURST

The beautiful Milk House in Sissinghurst is a former 16th-century hall house, with ancient timber beams and a Tudor fireplace. The menus use the freshest seasonal ingredients from local suppliers and the dishes are classic pub fare. The interior is beautifully styled and light with original features painted in soft chalky tones and pretty flowers embellishing the tables.

The outside gardens and terrace are the perfect place to spend summer lunches or late evening dinners under the stars. The terrace also features a wood-fired pizza oven serving homemade pizzas topped with delicious local charcuterie, cheeses and herbs. Local vineyards and microbreweries contribute to the drinks menu.

ADDRESS
The Street, Sissinghurst,
Cranbrook
TN17 2JG

PHONE
01580 720200

The Ram

BN8 6NS | SUSSEX | FIRLE

The Ram Inn has been at the heart of Firle village life for over 500 years. The rambling old brick and flint building has three main rooms, each with its own open fire, lit every day between October and April. Dark inky colours paint the walls and contrast against glittering chandeliers in the upstairs dining room.

The old stable and coach house have been converted into a private dining room and an outside 'farmers bar' where local dog walkers and horse riders enjoy a drink in the sunshine. An ancient flint-walled garden is ideal for sitting under the greengage trees in summer.

ADDRESS

29 The Street, West Firle,
Lewes
BN8 6NS

PHONE

01273 858222

Rye

The medieval town of Rye looks almost like a film-set in parts with lengthy cobbled streets and narrow passages. Overlooking Romney Marsh, this hill perched ancient town was originally located on a huge embayment of the English Channel and served as one of the fine Cinque Ports.

Arundel

Even from a distance Arundel is imposing and impressive; Gothic spires jut from the Cathedral, which overlooks the town and the picture-postcard castle can be seen over the low-lying marsh grounds and river Arun. The town centre has a variety of different eateries, independent shops, art spaces and antique stores.

Winchester

Winchester is a historically rich city on the western edge of the South Downs National Park. It was England's ancient capital and former seat of King Alfred the Great. Today the city retains its unique charm with many of the original buildings remaining as prominent features of the city centre.

Whitstable

Whitstable is renowned for its culinary excellence and pretty seaside charm. This seaside retreat is popular due to its sophisticated and contemporary approach to food and its attractive aesthetic. The town has been celebrated for its seafood since Roman times.

Lewes

Lewes is certainly one of Sussex's most attractive market towns and an ideal visitor destination. It is relatively small, yet filled with historic buildings such as Lewes Castle and the Anne of Cleves House. It's also home to Harvey's Brewery and a handful of their pubs.

Petworth

Petworth is a small, attractive market town set in the heart of the South Downs National Park. Known as a centre for arts and culture and home to more antique shops than any other in the South of England. Perfect for neophiles and traditionalists.

Hastings

Hastings is one of Sussex's finest seaside towns and is renowned for the famous 1066 battle. Noteworthy attractions include the Jerwood Gallery, East Cliff Railway and newly renovated pier. We suggest a visit to the Old Town for a rummage through the many antique shops, followed by a spot of lunch in The Crown.

Alfriston

Alfriston is one of the oldest villages in the country and for that reason, it's a popular spot for visitors. A plethora of historic buildings stretches along the high street and beyond to the parish church of St Andrews and famous Clergy House.

Canterbury

SOUTH EAST | PLACES WE LOVE |

Situated on the river Stour, the historic cathedral city of Canterbury is a UNESCO world heritage site. Occupied since Palaeolithic times, many historic architectural structures populate the area, including its landmark cathedral, the Roman city wall, a Norman castle and the ruins of St Augustine's Abbey.

Margate

SOUTH EAST | PLACES WE LOVE |

Margate's internationally acclaimed Turner Contemporary gallery, showcasing contemporary and historical art-works has put Margate back on the map. Previously known as a seaside holiday destination, the area is fast becoming an artistic centre with families also returning to its beaches after a period of regeneration.

Deal

SOUTH EAST | PLACES WE LOVE |

On a clear day, you can see France on the horizon from the town of Deal which is situated just 25 miles from the mainland. Deal was formerly a fishing, mining and garrison town and its position on the English Channel made it a significant and extremely busy port.

Folkestone

SOUTH EAST | PLACES WE LOVE |

Folkestone has undergone huge regeneration in recent years and is now an exciting hub for creatives and a wonderful town to visit. The Creative cobbled Quarter stretches upward from the sandy beach into the centre of town and includes a whole host of galleries, independent shops and stylish eateries.

Ventnor

SOUTH EAST | PLACES WE LOVE |

Ventnor is a traditional seaside resort built in the Victorian era which retains much of its original character. Ventnor has long been a magnet for writers, artists and other creatives, something that is still true today as the town has a vibrant art scene. The fine shingle beach slopes gently within a sheltered bay and beneath the tiered Victorian town.

Cowes

SOUTH EAST | PLACES WE LOVE |

Cowes is located on the West bank of the River Medina with the smaller town of East Cowes situated on the Eastern side. The two towns are connected by a chain ferry called the Cowes Floating Bridge. East Cowes is also noted as the favourite home of Queen Victoria, who lived at the splendid Osborne House.

Yarmouth

SOUTH EAST | PLACES WE LOVE |

Yarmouth is an historic port town located on the North West corner of the Isle of Wight and is so named for its location at the mouth of the River Western Yar. The town contains some of the oldest architecture on the Isle of Wight including a Grade II listed pier and a 16th-century castle.

Beaulieu

SOUTH EAST | PLACES WE LOVE |

Beaulieu is a small village on the South Eastern edge of the New Forest and at the head of the Beaulieu River. The name is French for "beautiful place", the village dates back to the 13th century and is centred around the abbey which was founded in 1204 by Cistercian monks.

Want the Pub Guide on your iPad?

The Best of England Pub Guide is also available to download as
a PDF to keep on your phone or iPad

Available now from
bestofengland.shop

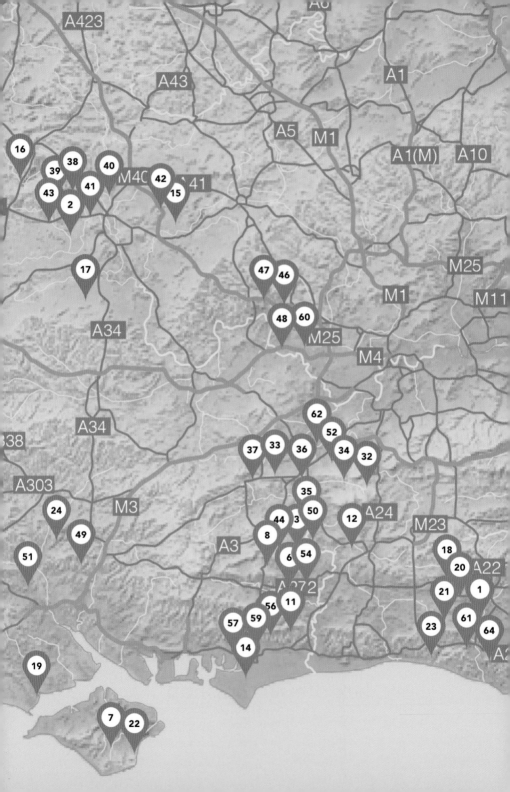

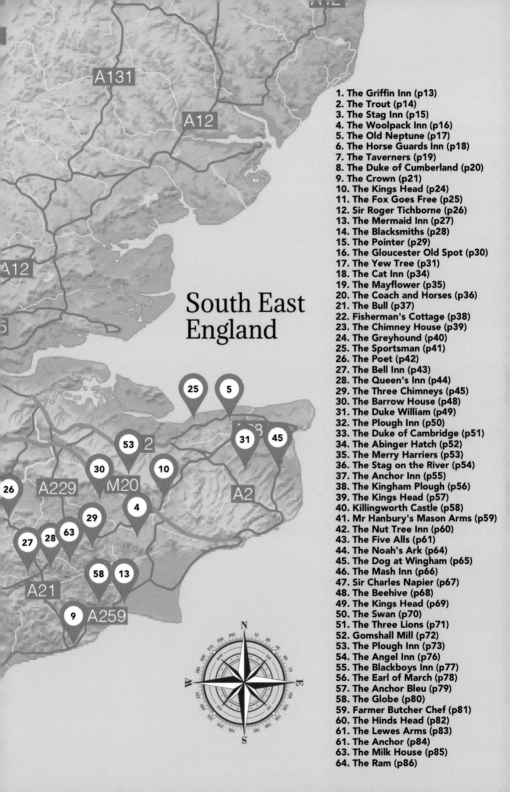

South East England

1. The Griffin Inn (p13)
2. The Trout (p14)
3. The Stag Inn (p15)
4. The Woolpack Inn (p16)
5. The Old Neptune (p17)
6. The Horse Guards Inn (p18)
7. The Taverners (p19)
8. The Duke of Cumberland (p20)
9. The Crown (p21)
10. The Kings Head (p24)
11. The Fox Goes Free (p25)
12. Sir Roger Tichborne (p26)
13. The Mermaid Inn (p27)
14. The Blacksmiths (p28)
15. The Pointer (p29)
16. The Gloucester Old Spot (p30)
17. The Yew Tree (p31)
18. The Cat Inn (p34)
19. The Mayflower (p35)
20. The Coach and Horses (p36)
21. The Bull (p37)
22. Fisherman's Cottage (p38)
23. The Chimney House (p39)
24. The Greyhound (p40)
25. The Sportsman (p41)
26. The Poet (p42)
27. The Bell Inn (p43)
28. The Queen's Inn (p44)
29. The Three Chimneys (p45)
30. The Barrow House (p48)
31. The Duke William (p49)
32. The Plough Inn (p50)
33. The Duke of Cambridge (p51)
34. The Abinger Hatch (p52)
35. The Merry Harriers (p53)
36. The Stag on the River (p54)
37. The Anchor Inn (p55)
38. The Kingham Plough (p56)
39. The Kings Head (p57)
40. Killingworth Castle (p58)
41. Mr Hanbury's Mason Arms (p59)
42. The Nut Tree Inn (p60)
43. The Five Alls (p61)
44. The Noah's Ark (p64)
45. The Dog at Wingham (p65)
46. The Mash Inn (p66)
47. Sir Charles Napier (p67)
48. The Beehive (p68)
49. The Kings Head (p69)
50. The Swan (p70)
51. The Three Lions (p71)
52. Gomshall Mill (p72)
53. The Plough Inn (p73)
54. The Angel Inn (p76)
55. The Blackboys Inn (p77)
56. The Earl of March (p78)
57. The Anchor Bleu (p79)
58. The Globe (p80)
59. Farmer Butcher Chef (p81)
60. The Hinds Head (p82)
61. The Lewes Arms (p83)
61. The Anchor (p84)
63. The Milk House (p85)
64. The Ram (p86)

CHAPTER THREE

SOUTH
WEST

The Pandora Inn

TR11 5ST | **CORNWALL** | FALMOUTH

Few pubs can claim to serve fish fresh from the boat, but Falmouth's 13th-century Pandora Inn does. But that's not the only thing that makes this inn special. Home to a cosy, character bar and restaurant, you can hunker down on a blustery day and enjoy food by the fire. When the sun shines, the pub's floating pontoon becomes the star of the show with meals served on the water.

The experience is relaxed, with coffee and cake kicking off proceedings in the morning, followed by a series of locally sourced daily specials and traditional coastal dishes. St Austell's Brewery ales, Cornish Orchards' cider and Tarquin's local gin stock the bar with local drinks.

ADDRESS

Restronguet Creek, Mylor Bridge, Falmouth TR11 5ST

PHONE

01326 372678

The Gurnard's Head

TR26 3DE | **CORNWALL** | ST. IVES

A landmark pub almost at the edge of England, the Gurnard's Head is your last stop for a pint and an open fire before the Atlantic Ocean. Between St Just and Zennor, this is genuine Cornwall. Wild, mysterious and beautiful, the Gurnard's Head is an inn that transports you back to when travel was that little bit slower.

With excellent dining and rooms with comfortable beds, the Gurnard's Head is both a welcome stop-off and a destination in itself. The food is simple, fresh, local wherever possible and of exceptional quality. As such, this pub regularly features in national pub guides and has a loyal following.

ADDRESS

Nr Zennor, St. Ives, Penzance
TR26 3DE

PHONE

01736 796928

The Port William

PL34 0HB | **CORNWALL** | TINTAGEL

A cut above many Cornish inns, The Port William makes the most of its coastal location with floor-to-ceiling glazing in the restaurant, framing vast Atlantic views. Already a hotspot with surfers, you can enjoy a meal by the sea on a sunny day or cosy up and watch the lashing waves from a comfy spot beside the toasty wood burner.

The menu is a celebration of Cornwall, from comfort food classics to the finest seafood catches. The coffee is brewed to the pub's own recipe and the bar is kept well stocked. With eight family and dog-friendly four-star rooms, stroll along the beach, fill your boots and then doze off to the sound of the sea.

ADDRESS

Tintagel Heights, Trebarwith
PL34 0HB

PHONE

01840 770230

The Compasses Inn

SP3 6NB | WILTSHIRE | TISBURY

The Compasses Inn delivers on every expectation of a traditional Wiltshire pub. It's steeped in history, dating back to the 14th-century and indulges idyllic visions of country life. Settling down beside the inglenook fireplace with the manager's renowned Bloody Mary or a pint of Butcombe Ale, you could imagine doing the same a hundred years earlier.

But The Compasses hasn't stood still. In fact, the menu changes daily to showcase the freshest seasonal ingredients in an unpretentious style within the inn's homely, historic surrounds. The bar never runs dry, with a selection of European wines and new beers appearing on a regular basis. Modern touches can also be found in the inn's four country bedrooms and self-catering Plum Cottage.

ADDRESS
Lower Chicksgrove, Tisbury
SP3 6NB

PHONE
01722 714318

The Wheatsheaf

BA2 7EG | SOMERSET | BATH

The Wheatsheaf was originally a farmhouse built in 1576 and parts of the present building date back to the 16th century. Today the pub preserves the best of its past, with its beautiful interior features whilst enhancing its contemporary style and exceptional approach to food, serving only the very best of local and home-grown produce.

The cosy open log fire is a welcome addition in the cooler Autumn and Winter months whilst the terrace and garden come alive in the spring and summer. Country chic transcends the menu, dining area and beautifully appointed bedrooms. Glamping with exceptional views and luxurious facilities can be booked here too.

ADDRESS

Combe Hay Lane, Bath
BA2 7EG

PHONE

01225 833504

English Vineyards

10 of the best...

1. *Rathfinny Wine Estate, Sussex*
2. *Camel Valley, Cornwall*
3. *Hush Heath Estate, Kent*
4. *Wyken Vineyards, Suffolk*
5. *Ryedale Vineyards, Yorkshire*
6. *Three Choirs Vineyard, Gloucestershire*
7. *Ridgeview Wine Estate, Sussex*
8. *Setley Ridge, Hampshire*
9. *Knightor Winery, Cornwall*
10. *Chapel Down, Kent*

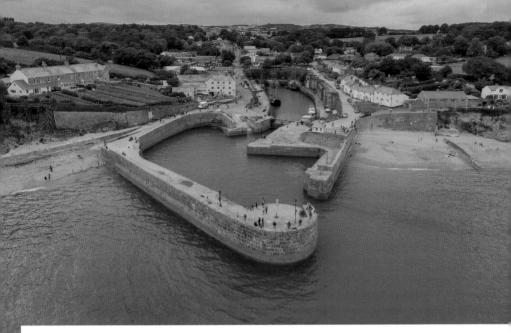

The Pier House

PL25 3NJ | ST AUSTELL | CHARLESTOWN

The Pier House's position beside the bay is a charming one and the bustling harbour offers a quaint view from the terrace or seats inside. A stone chimney, parquet flooring and more than one nod to the nautical give the pub distinctive coastal appeal. The dining area is relaxed, but with a more refined feel – an authentic setting to enjoy the pub's locally sourced produce.

With the sea on the doorstep and attractions like the Lost Gardens of Heligan nearby, visitors can make use of the 27 comfortable and neutrally decorated rooms as they explore more of Cornwall's coastline.

ADDRESS

Harbour Front, Charlestown
PL25 3NJ

PHONE

01726 67955

The Ebrington Arms

GL55 6NH | **GLOUCESTERSHIRE** | CHIPPING CAMPDEN

Once voted the UK's favourite pub, The Ebrington Arms has oodles of country appeal. Visitors will love the honey-stone walls covered in wisteria, spacious garden for sunny days and quiet village setting, under 10 minutes from the sought-after Cotswolds town of Chipping Campden. The menu is hearty, warming and features plenty of pub favourites, earning it AA rosette acclaim.

Renovated by the current owners, the pub is as much a hotspot for locals as it is a destination, a tradition the inn has proudly continued for nearly 400 years. But, if you are visiting from further afield, The Ebrington Arms has five luxurious rooms with which to welcome you. Each comes with homemade biscuits, a boozy nightcap and quaint Cotswolds views.

ADDRESS

May Lane, Ebrington, Chipping Campden

GL55 6NH

PHONE

01386 593223

The Rock Inn

TQ13 9XP | DEVON | DARTMOOR NATIONAL PARK

In the breath-taking Dartmoor National Park, The Rock Inn has been earning AA rosettes for over two decades. Timber beams, antique furniture and cosy features give the inn all the welcome trimmings of an intimate country pub. Locally grown, reared and caught meat, fish and produce make it onto the plates here in contemporary combinations. The food is so successful that the restaurant is often booked out.

The inn has its beginnings in the 19th century and has welcomed locals and visitors in the 200 years since then. The en-suite bedrooms, furnished with antiques, make The Rock Inn an excellent Dartmoor base to this very day.

ADDRESS

Haytor Vale, Dartmoor National Park

TQ13 9XP

PHONE

01364 661305

The Ship Inn

TR19 6QX | CORNWALL | MOUSEHOLE

Full of Cornish character and charm, the Ship Inn in Mousehole is a friendly pub with eight comfortable rooms offering splendid views of the sea and quaint Mousehole harbour. The bar and restaurant serve fresh local food all year round and the traditional Cornish pub food is accompanied by the excellent St. Austell ales.

The pub's position gives them great access to some of the finest fish in the British Isles and their home cooking truly has the taste of Cornwall in every dish. Low ceilings, wooden beams and open fires add to the cosy character.

ADDRESS

South Cliff, Mousehole
TR19 6QX

PHONE

01736 731234

The George Townhouse

CV36 4AJ | WARWICKSHIRE | SHIPSTON-ON-STOUR

The George house in Shipston is an attractively spacious modern pub with 15 luxurious rooms and fine cuisine. In 2016 it received an extensive makeover that has transformed it into the destination pub it is today. From breakfast through to dinner the standard of food is top-notch, with decent service to match.

Multiple dining spaces allow diners to opt for a more casual or formal meal depending on their preference and the patio out the back is perfect for long summer evenings. Their menus are far from meat-focused, with plenty of options for vegetarians and those intolerant to gluten. The George is fantastically situated in the centre of Shipston, bordering the Cotswolds and Warwickshire.

ADDRESS

8 High Street, Shipston-on-Stour

CV36 4AJ

PHONE

01608 661453

The Blue Peter Inn

PL13 2QZ | CORNWALL | POLPERRO

Sitting on the harbour wall of the stunning village of Polperro, the Blue Peter Inn offers a warm welcome to all comers. They offer great beer, food, superb views and live music for which its fame has spread far and wide. They do their best to ensure the journey from the sea to your plate is a short one which isn't difficult given their location.

Supporting and developing the local music scene is an important part of what the Blue Peter Inn stands for, which makes this a vibrant venue to spend an evening. As a free house, the Blue Peter offers an eclectic mix of real ales, ciders and lagers along with mulled wine in the winter months.

ADDRESS
Quay Road, Polperro, Bodmin
PL13 2QZ

PHONE
01503 272743

English Breweries

10 of the best...

1. National Brewery Centre, Staffordshire
2. Hook Norton Brewery, Oxfordshire
3. Northern Monk, Leeds
4. Adnams, Suffolk
5. St Austell, Cornwall
6. Hawkshead, Cumbria
7. Shepherd Neame, Kent
8. Palmers Brewery, Dorset
9. The Three Tuns, Shropshire
10. Harveys Brewery, Sussex

The Museum Inn

DT11 8DE | DORSET | NR BLANDFORD FORUM

The Museum Inn's sleepy, country style with character red brick walls and a thatched roof make the forward-thinking menu served inside an exciting surprise. The fare is seasonal and contemporary, a striking contrast to the inn's character interior. It's ideal for tourists and locals alike because the seasonality means the dishes won't stay the same for long.

After dinner, pull up a stool and enjoy a local ale at the bar, hunker down beside the open fire or retire to one of the inn's eight sumptuous, en-suite bedrooms. There's also the self-catering Mole's Cottage next door. With room for 16 to stay, it makes an excellent base for larger gatherings, with Stonehenge and Lulworth Cove in easy reach.

ADDRESS

Farnham, Nr Blandford Forum
DT11 8DE

PHONE

01725 516261

The Bearslake Inn

EX20 4HQ | **DEVON** | OKEHAMPTON

The Bearslake Inn in Lake Sourton is a traditional, Grade II listed thatched roof pub nestled within the beautiful North West corner of Dartmoor. Bear or be-re comes from the old Devon word meaning wooded place and Lake is the hamlet where the farm is located, so the original name may have meant the wooded place in Lake. The original building is a Devon Longhouse which provided shelter to people and animals alike. Parts of this particular one are thought to date back to the 13th Century.

Today, the pub is a welcoming, family-run establishment which is well worth stopping off at for a refreshment or bite to eat.

ADDRESS

Lake, Sourton, Okehampton
EX20 4HQ

PHONE

01837 861334

The Golden Lion

PL29 3RB | **CORNWALL** | **PORT ISAAC**

This 18th-century pub in Port Isaac is awash with charm and history. Overlooking the stunning bay makes this an ideal spot to watch the beautiful blues of summer calm and the dramatic greys of winter storms. The Golden Lion takes pride in their cask ale and serves a fine fish and chips.

The Golden Lion has an interesting and rich seafaring history and is home to the 'Bloody Bones Bar' which houses a smuggling tunnel leading onto a causeway on the beach. Sit in front of a fire and enjoy the exceptional views over this magnificent Cornish harbour whilst enjoying the local seafood.

ADDRESS

10 Fore Street, Port Isaac
PL29 3RB

PHONE

01208 880336

The Ship Inn

PL27 6DF | CORNWALL | WADEBRIDGE

The Ship Inn's position gives it great access to some of the finest fish in the British Isles and its home cooking truly has the taste of Cornwall in every dish. Low ceilings, wooden beams and open fires add to the cosy character.

This is a straightforward Cornish pub and a fine one at that. The focus is on community and, as such, is a hit with the locals. The menu consists of simple pub grub made with local ingredients which is updated daily. Try the catch of the day from nearby Newlyn fish market.

ADDRESS
Gonvena Hill, Wadebridge
PL27 6DF

PHONE
01208 813845

The Old Custom House

PL28 8BL | CORNWALL | PADSTOW

Nestled within the harbour town of Padstow is the Old Custom House, a B&B and restaurant known for its excellent quality and service. There is a stylish and intimate bar along with comfortable guest rooms and a well-equipped spa. The Old Custom House directly overlooks the bustling harbour and sits in the midst of all of the hustle and bustle.

Food and drinks range from freshly brewed fair trade coffee and local ales to fresh Cornish shellfish. The Old Custom House strives to provide the best local food served in a home-cooked way and will rarely disappoint.

ADDRESS

South Quay, Padstow
PL28 8BL

PHONE

01841 532359

The Star & Garter

TR11 2AF | **CORNWALL** | FALMOUTH

The Star and Garter is a 19th-century pub with a distinctly contemporary menu. It can't be beaten for its views over Falmouth harbour from where they receive most of their fish. The meat served at the Star is also cured and smoked on the premises.

The highlight of the week is the Sunday roast but the combined talents of the chefs always produce something special every day of the week. The Star isn't just about food - its long list of whiskeys and rums are matched by sprightly and creative cocktails. They also have two apartments which continue the heritage nautical theme of the pub.

ADDRESS

52 High Street, Falmouth
TR11 2AF

PHONE

01326 316663

The Millbrook Inn

TQ7 2RW | **DEVON** | **KINGSBRIDGE**

Situated in the village of South Pool in the heart of the South Hams, this idyllic spot can also be reached by boat from Salcombe when the tide is right. It is easy to reach from the local towns of Kingsbridge and Dartmouth.

Jean-Phillippe Bidart their award-winning chef, heads up the Millbrook Inn kitchen, bringing his unique, Gallic sensibility to their local and seasonal menu. Low beams, roaring fires and original stone wall features make this a popular and traditional choice.

ADDRESS

South Pool, Kingsbridge
TQ7 2RW

PHONE

01548 531581

The King John Inn

SP5 5PS | WILTSHIRE | SALISBURY

Hearty, homemade fare in a heritage setting, The King John Inn on the border of Wiltshire and Dorset is a destination in its own right. Relax into a Chesterfield sofa or wander through the Victorian tiered gardens with a drink to start, then take a seat in the rustic restaurant for the main event.

Priding themselves on an award-winning menu inspired by their proximity to both land and sea, if you're game for some Great British classics, this could be the pub for you. The bar is equally refreshing, serving different beverages every week and there are eight, dog-friendly bedrooms filled with antiques waiting upstairs.

ADDRESS
Tollard Royal, Salisbury
SP5 5PS

PHONE
01725 516207

The Old Stocks Inn

GL54 1AF | GLOUCESTERSHIRE | STOW-ON-THE-WOLD

A hidden gem in the Cotswolds, The Old Stocks Inn is an enchanting fusion of new and old. Inside the honey-stone, 17th-century walls, suspended light bulbs hang beside centuries-old beams and retro, colour block chairs contrast restored stone. The team has built a menu to match, with artisan coffees, locally sourced ingredients and a quirky café to boot.

The renovated inn pedals a 'home from home' experience if you book one of its quirky rooms, but if our homes were that nice, we wouldn't need to go away. There are 16 to choose from, including family and dog-friendly options so you can make Stow on the Wold your boutique Cotswolds' base.

ADDRESS

The Square, Stow-on-the-Wold
GL54 1AF

PHONE

01451 830666

The Tinner's Arms

TR26 3BY | CORNWALL | ST. IVES

The Tinner's Arms is a traditional pub that is the beating heart of Zennor and is one of Cornwall's hidden gems. This Grade II listed, 13th-century pub has stone floors, low ceilings and inglenook fireplaces.

At the centre of the village for over 700 years, the pub has provided welcoming refuge, a roaring fire and a fine pint of ale ever since. First built for the masons working on the church of Saint Senara in the village, this is still the only pub in Zennor and as in the past, the food is hearty, satisfying and locally sourced.

ADDRESS
Zennor, St. Ives
TR26 3BY

PHONE
01736 796927

The Farmers' Market

10 of the best....

Ashton Farmers' Market - North West
Last Sunday of the month 9am - 2pm

Moseley Farmers' Market - West Midlands
Last Saturday of the month 9am - 2pm

Totnes Good Food Market - South Downs
Every Sunday 10am

Alnwick Farmers' Market - North East
Every Saturday 9am - 4pm

Winchester Farmers Market - Hampshire
Every Sunday 9am - 2pm

Orton Farmers' Market - Cumbria
2nd Saturday of every month

St Ives Farmers' Market - Cornwall
Every Thursday 9:30am - 2pm

The Good Shed - Kent
Tuesday - Sunday

Lavenham Farmers' Market - Suffolk
Last Sunday of the month 10am - 2pm

Bakewell Farmers' Market - Derbyshire
Last Saturday of the month 9am - 2pm

The Inn at Cranborne

BH21 5PP | DORSET | WIMBORNE

This Dorset inn has over 400 years of history to its name, having first opened its doors in the 16th-century. Since then, The Inn at Cranborne has proudly welcomed locals and travellers, including writer Thomas Hardy, in its picturesque location on Cranborne Chase, close to the New Forest. Today, the inn is awash with cosy, country features, from flagstone floors and oak beams to atmospheric, wood-panelled walls.

Diners can choose between several different rooms, including the Lamp Room for larger groups. The dedicated kitchen team prepare seasonal menus, making the most of locally caught fish, cheese and produce. They cure their own salmon in-house and grow their own in their kitchen garden.

ADDRESS

5 Wimborne Street, Wimborne
BH21 5PP

PHONE

01725 551249

The Seagrave Arms

GL55 6QH | GLOUCESTERSHIRE | CHIPPING CAMPDEN

The Cotswolds are at the heart of what Chipping Campden's The Seagrave Arms offers. Local gin, local ales, local ingredients, grown, cooked and eaten in the same Cotswolds countryside – it's an appealing proposition made even greater by the pub's curb appeal. Boasting Georgian proportions clad with Cotswolds' stone, it seems the pub's present-day ethos was woven into the building centuries ago.

You can eat inside or out at this award-winning inn, with a private garden and cosy fire pit making the beer garden appealing year-round. Make a weekend of your visit and book one of the eight uniquely furnished bedrooms – go for the four-poster room if you're celebrating.

ADDRESS
Friday Street, Weston Subedge, GL55 6QH

PHONE
01386 840192

The Howard Arms

CV36 4LT | WARWICKSHIRE | ILMINGTON

A relaxed country pub, The Howard Arms is Ilmington's hub and overlooks the quaint village green. Living up to every expectation of a country idyll, flower-laden window boxes pepper the exterior while chunky flagstone floors, open fires and deep, comfy armchairs await in the bar.

The bread is baked fresh daily, ingredients come from the surrounding Cotswolds countryside and, if you stay the night in one of the eight charming rooms, breakfast is three courses! The Howard Arms is a classic inn with a luxurious twist and with Stratford-upon-Avon only eight miles away, it's well worth a visit.

ADDRESS
Lower Green, Ilmington
CV36 4LT

PHONE
01608 682226

The Blisland Inn

PL30 4JK | **CORNWALL** | **BODMIN**

Having served over 1,370 real ales since opening The Blisland Inn, husband and wife team Gary and Margaret Marshall would be justified in renaming this pub the Bodmin Moor boozer. You only need to enter the bar to see the walls covered in ale paraphernalia and it won't be long before a hand-pulled drink is in your hand. It's an eclectic, lively setting where a friendly greeting is guaranteed.

In keeping with the pub's traditional appeal, the menu is home-cooked and honest, leaning towards British comfort food classics – just what you need after a hike on the moor. Only 15 minutes from the infamous Jamaica Inn and 30 from Port Isaac, there's plenty to see and do nearby.

ADDRESS

Blisland, Bodmin
PL30 4JK

PHONE

01208 850739

The Butchers Arms

GL19 4NX | GLOUCESTERSHIRE | ELDERSFIELD

The Butchers Arms is a charming country pub in the Gloucestershire countryside of Michelin-starred fame. Run by husband and wife team, Mark and Jo-Anne Block carefully balance their culinary offering with the needs of the loyal crowd of locals who regularly meet for a drink. As such, sitting down to eat here is a far from stuffy experience. On the contrary, the atmosphere buzzes with greetings and conversation in cosy, character surrounds as patrons sample the day's cask-served ale.

The menu itself showcases Ingredients that are seasonal but surprising. The result is excellent pub food, but not always as you'd expect it.

ADDRESS

Lime Street, Eldersfield
GL19 4NX

PHONE

01452 840381

The Lion Inn

GL54 5PS | **GLOUCESTERSHIRE** | WINCHCOMBE

Half an hour from Cheltenham, The Lion Inn in Winchcombe heralds a true Cotswolds retreat. The 15th-century coaching inn underwent a sympathetic renovation in 2011 and is now home to a rustic restaurant, cosy snug and comfortable bedrooms, with quirky character features.

Taking an innovative approach to local produce, this pub will even exchange local growers a drink for any spare allotment or garden vegetables. The award-winning menu changes frequently and is filled with seasonal and locally sourced British dishes. Nearby, Sudeley Castle & Gardens are well worth exploring.

ADDRESS
37 North Street, Winchcombe
GL54 5PS

PHONE
01242 603300

The Slaughters Country Inn

GL54 2HS | GLOUCESTERSHIRE | CHELTENHAM

You'd be hard-pushed to find a more picturesque location than Upper and Lower Slaughter in the Cotswolds and it's in the latter that you'll find The Slaughters Country Inn. This traditional inn welcomes walkers in their droves, as well as local residents and hotel guests.

The menu is local, seasonal and simple and can be enjoyed in the idyllic garden or inside, where you'll find bookcases filled to the brim with novels and board games to enjoy – the perfect accompaniment to lunch on a rainy day. For special occasions, traditional cream teas and afternoon teas are served in the lounge or on the terrace, with 31 indulgent bedrooms should you wish to make a weekend of it.

ADDRESS

Lower Slaughter, Cheltenham
GL54 2HS

PHONE

01451 822143

The Hare and Hounds

BA1 5TJ | SOMERSET | BATH

With some of the finest views over Bath's spectacular countryside, the Hare & Hounds is a tranquil spot to enjoy breathtaking views from their terrace, whilst indulging in their popular menus, created using local produce.

Abundant lavender bushes and wildflowers scent the pathway to the pub and once inside the dining room, the awe-inspiring view from the enormous stone and lead window makes its impact. Natural light floods into this stylish room with dark wood floors, high ceilings, white walls and accents of chalky blue.

ADDRESS
Landsdown Road, Bath
BA1 5TJ

PHONE
01225 482682

Fresh Crab

It's easy to forget that England is, in fact, part of an island, but don't let the less than tropical temperatures blind you to the gastronomic treasures to be found in our cool, coastal waters.

It's estimated that there are 65 species of crab alone and while you can't eat them all, soft flakes of crab flesh taste superb when served with a sweet chilli kick.

The Amberley Inn

GL5 5AF | GLOUCESTERSHIRE | AMBERLEY

The Amberley Inn is perched on the corner of the quaint Cotswolds village that gives the pub its name. Rolling countryside extends in every direction, making it a hub for walkers descending from the hills of Minchinhampton Common. Mullioned windows, golden stone and parquet flooring pay homage to the inn's 19th century past.

You can eat in both the character bar and the more refined restaurant. The menu is fantastically fresh, stocked by daily deliveries from local suppliers including beef and lamb produced on Gatcombe Park Estate. The inn also features 13 modern rooms. Country shows, horse trials and other outdoor events take place close by.

ADDRESS

Culver Hill, Amberley
GL5 5AF

PHONE

01453 872565

The Royal Oak

GL8 8EY | GLOUCESTERSHIRE | TETBURY

The Royal Oak in the ever-popular Cotswolds village of Tetbury has been lovingly restored. Now, the inn is a thriving base that serves the local village well in its character bar and dining room. Creating a beguiling balance between old and new, a serve-yourself Bloody Mary station brings the historic bar bang up to date. In the beamed dining room, organic food and pub classics make an appealing menu.

Tetbury is home to a sought-after selection of shops, ranging from antiques to boutique homewares. The six en-suite bedrooms at The Royal Oak provide a comfortable, country base from which to explore.

ADDRESS
1 Cirencester Road, Tetbury
GL8 8EY

PHONE
01666 500021

The Red Lion Inn

SN6 6DD | WILTSHIRE | CRICKLADE

At the heart of Cricklade's high street, you'll find The Red Lion Inn, which has been the locals' boozer of choice since the 1600s. But while the building retains its character features and purpose of old, one glance at the beer menu unearths a modern surprise. Since 2012, the inn has expanded to include its own on-site brewery, known as The Hop Kettle Brewery. You can try their beers at the bar, alongside an exciting line-up of smoked beer, bitters, pale ales, stouts and ciders.

But it's not only about the booze. The food is award-winning and hearty and The Red Lion Inn also offers five en-suite bedrooms, two of which are dog-friendly, allowing you to make the most of the nearby Cotswolds and North Wessex Downs.

ADDRESS

74 High Street, Cricklade
SN6 6DD

PHONE

01793 750776

The Castle Inn

SN14 7HN | WILTSHIRE | CASTLE COMBE

This Wiltshire pub has an enviable waterfront position in the enchanting Cotswold village of Castle Combe. Dating back to the 12th-century, the inn has been elegantly restored to make the most of its heritage stonework and charming features, while providing a taste of country luxury to please patrons of today.

Take a seat out the front or on the terrace for lunch and watch the world go by as billowing hanging baskets sway in the breeze, then enjoy a meandering walk along the burbling river. The bar is incredibly inviting with stone walls and an open fire, teamed with a menu of British classics to match. Make a weekend of it with a stay in The Castle Inn's 12 luxurious bedrooms.

ADDRESS

Castle Combe
SN14 7HN

PHONE

01249 783030

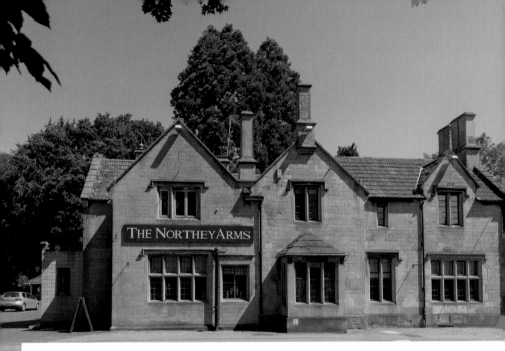

The Northey Arms

SN13 8AE | **WILTSHIRE** | CORSHAM

The Northey Arms is a beautiful honey-coloured stone pub close to the city of Bath with an imposing exterior. Steeped in history, having been frequented in the past by the world-famous English Playwright Noel Coward, the interiors are contemporary and light and the menu is locally renowned.

Having received Michelin and AA recognition, culinary excellence is the focus in the kitchen, where each ingredient is sourced through exhaustive research of local suppliers directed by Development Chef, Ross Harper. The freshest fish from Cornish Shores regularly appear on the menu and they additionally stock a great range of ciders, lagers and real ales and considered wine list to complement.

ADDRESS

Bath Road, Corsham
SN13 8AE

PHONE

01225 742333

The Feathered Nest

OX7 6SD | **OXFORDSHIRE** | CHIPPING NORTON

The Feathered Nest is a former Malthouse, refurbished from the ground up in 2009 to become the family-run inn that it is today. Located on the Gloucestershire-Oxfordshire border, 20 minutes from the ever-popular town of Chipping Norton, the pub now enjoys a fine reputation that has earned it three AA rosettes.

The menu focuses on seasonal ingredients, working with local suppliers as much as possible. Indulge your inner sommelier, as well as your stomach, with The Feathered Nest's 240-bin strong wine list. You can also hop into the saddle at the bar to savour a cask ale pint or warm up on a winter's day beside the log fire.

ADDRESS

Nether Westcote, Chipping Norton

OX7 6SD

PHONE

01993 833030

The Marlborough Tavern

BA1 2LY | SOMERSET | BATH

The Marlborough Tavern is a pub with stripped back elegance in the heart of Bath. With an emphasis on quality local and seasonal food, the pub is situated in a golden-hued Bath Stone building with an outside terrace.

Evenings at The Marlborough Tavern are candlelit with tables outside embraced by ancient stone walls, flagstone floors and surrounded by wooden troughs filled with lavender. Inside the pared back interior creates a contemporary style with an emphasis on the renowned cuisine.

ADDRESS

35 Marlborough Buildings, Bath
BA1 2LY

PHONE

01225 423731

The Bell

SN8 2PE | WILTSHIRE | RAMSBURY

The Bell is an award-winning pub in Ramsbury near Marlborough. Head chef Jonas Lodge sources as much as possible from their kitchen garden and the wider Ramsbury Estate, ensuring the cuisine is fresh and inspired by the seasons. The interior reflects the country classic spirit of the menu, with roaring fires, wooden floors and comfortable seating.

The ingredients really matter here and they work closely with specialist partners to provide the finest produce, such as their line-caught fish which arrives daily from Cornwall. Bedrooms are contemporary and carefully designed with luxurious details for extra comfort.

The Square, Ramsbury
SN8 2PE

PHONE

01672 520230

The Pony and Trap

BS40 8TQ | BRISTOL | CHEW MAGNA

The Pony & Trap in Chew Magna has held a Michelin Star since 2011 and was ranked 2nd in the Estrella Damm Top 50 UK Gastropubs in 2018. The "field to fork" ethos of the pub ensures that ingredients are sourced as locally as possible from suppliers around the Chew Valley and the South West.

Brother and sister Josh and Holly lead a talented team of chefs, wine experts and waiting staff, serving up food and drinks from the very best growers and producers in the region and their reputation is justified. The light and rustic interior fuses beautiful views with original flagstone and parquet floors.

ADDRESS

New, Chew Magna
BS40 8TQ

PHONE

01275 332627

The St Tudy Inn

PL30 3NN | CORNWALL | BODMIN

Simple food served exceptionally. A charming village pub, The St Tudy Inn's seasonal menu has earned it Michelin acclaim that travels far beyond Cornwall's borders. It is executive chef Emily Scott's passion that propels this inn onto the culinary map, with ingredients echoing the seasons and making the most of what land and sea can produce.

Inside, the pub is as stylish as the food, with antique furniture, a roaring log burner and a leather armchair or two. The eponymous St Tudy Ale is brewed locally and the 12-strong cocktail and mocktail list is well worth a tipple or two. The inn also offers four double bedrooms in the converted barn, with the inn's own sausages served at breakfast.

ADDRESS
St Tudy, Bodmin
PL30 3NN

PHONE
01208 850656

Fish & Chips

Crisp, crunchy beer batter encasing delicate, moist white fish, served with a generous helping of thickly cut chips and a side of crushed peas – fish and chips is one of Britain's best comfort foods and is believed to date back over 150 years.

The white fish is typically cod or haddock, served up in cosy pubs or as a take-away traditionally wrapped in paper.

10 of the best

1. Millers Fish & Chips, Haxby,
2. Fylde Fish Bar, Southport
3. The Golden Carp Chippy, Redditch
4. Burton Road Chippy, Lincoln
5. Henley's of Wivenhoe, Wivenhoe
6. Captain's Fish and Chips, Hoddesdon
7. Harbourside Fish & Chips, Plymouth
8. The Magpie, Whitby
9. The Golden Galleon, Aldeburgh
10. Godfrey's, Harpenden

The Litton

BA3 4PW | **SOMERSET** | NEAR WELLS

The Litton is a beautiful and sympathetically restored, award-winning country pub and boutique hotel. Menus are inspired by the seasons and by local, sustainable ingredients. The cuisine fuses modern British highlights with influences from continental Europe

The stylish interior and en-suite rooms are individually designed to showcase the vintage and boutique style of the building and its history, with high ceilings, original exposed wooden beams, stone interior walls and period windows juxtaposed next to vibrant graphic prints, rustic textures and luxurious details.

ADDRESS

Litton, Near Wells
BA3 4PW

PHONE

01761 241 554

The Old Swan

OX29 ORN | **OXFORDSHIRE** | MINSTER LOVELL

The Old Swan & Minster Mill is an exceptional, quintessential country inn and boutique hotel in the heart of Oxfordshire. Beamed ceilings, roaring log fires and rugged flag-stone floors feature next to luxuriously classic interiors. The outdoor terrace and picturesque gardens are a treat during the summer months.

Expect fresh local, flavoursome ingredients and hearty dishes; from a pie and pint by the fireside in the colder months, or a salad on the terrace in the summer. The menu is seasonal and the food is simple and delicious. The Garden Spa offers hotel guests a tranquil and indulgent haven in the heart of the beautiful grounds.

ADDRESS

Old Minster, Minster Lovell
OX29 ORN

PHONE

01993 774441

The Lion

OX25 2PW | OXFORDSHIRE | WENDLEBURY

The Lion at Wendlebury is a beautiful Cotswold stone 18th-century pub in Oxfordshire with an emphasis on using the highest quality, locally-sourced ingredients. The light and contemporary interior showcases a blazing log fire, original features and a cosy ambience.

Daily deliveries from the best local, free-range and artisan producers dictate the regularly changing menu which naturally stays in line with the seasons. The bedrooms at The Lion at Wendlebury are beautifully appointed with a contemporary country chic style.

ADDRESS

Wendlebury Road, Bicester
OX25 2PW

PHONE

01869 388228

The Redan Inn

BA3 4HA | SOMERSET | CHILCOMPTON

Nestled into the old village of Chilcompton, The Redan Inn has been lovingly refurbished and has since been returned to its historical status as an Inn. With a sophisticated bar hosting a gin collection of over 100 bottles, local ales and international lagers, the interior is light with accents of inky blue and dark wood, a cosy wood-burner and candlelight.

The kitchen team has great ambition led by talented Chef Daniel Edwards, who works with the best locally sourced ingredients including those from their kitchen garden, producing dishes that have gained and maintained a two AA* rosette rating for 2018. Combined with Proprietor Toby Gritten's field-to-fork and foraging style of cookery, this team looks set to lead The Redan onto further accolades.

ADDRESS

Fry's Well, Chilcompton
BA3 4HA

PHONE

01761 258 560

The Talbot Inn

BA11 3PN | SOMERSET | FROME

The Talbot Inn in the village of Mells is a stylish pub situated in a historic and traditional 15th century inn. There is a main bar, snug, courtyard and map room which are all open every day for classic pub food and drink. Upstairs there are eight classically elegant bedrooms with crisp Egyptian cotton sheets, smart TVs and roll top baths.

Separated by a cobbled courtyard is the 500-year-old Sitting Room, Coach House Grill Room and a pretty garden. In the Coach House Grill Room, food is simply grilled over a charcoal and wood fire in the way country inns cooked hundreds of years ago. Menus at The Talbot Inn change with the season and obviously use local ingredients where possible, ensuring the best produce, some of which is grown in their own kitchen garden.

ADDRESS

Selwood Street, Frome
BA11 3PN

PHONE

01444 455898

The Beckford Arms

SP3 6PX | **WILTSHIRE** | TISBURY

The Beckford Arms is a traditional country pub infused with contemporary style, located on the edge of the stunning rolling parkland of the Fonthill Estate in south Wiltshire close to Stonehenge and Salisbury. The menus are seasonal and use local ingredients where possible, supporting local growers and ensuring the best produce, some of which is grown in their own kitchen garden.

The Sitting Room is classic in style with a soft colour palette of greys and features high ceilings, large bay windows and a roaring fire. On Sunday nights the pub often shows a classic movie in here. A selection of daily papers, monthly magazines and books from the library are also available to read in the bay window overlooking the Fonthill Estate. Eight bedrooms of differing sizes are luxurious and elegant.

ADDRESS

Fonthill Gifford, Tisbury
SP3 6PX

PHONE

01747 870385

The Royal Oak

SP3 5PA | WILTSHIRE | SALISBURY

Tucked away in the Nadder Valley, The Royal Oak has been an inn since 1852. The pub is set in the beautiful village of Swallowcliffe and nestled in a little dell. A recent refurbishment has created a beautiful mix of old and new, with traditional thick beams and stone fireplaces as well as stylish wooden furniture by local designer Matthew Burt and an on-trend colour palette.

Proudly supporting local farmers and growers, the cuisine is seasonal with ever-changing menus to accommodate this. The interior feels stylish and relaxed with its roaring fire, stone floors, light walls and natural wood. Bedrooms give the appearance of a boutique hotel with carefully considered details and a country chic aesthetic.

ADDRESS

Swallowcliffe, Salisbury
SP3 5PA

PHONE

01747 870211

The Red Lion

SN9 6AQ | **WILTSHIRE** | **PEWSEY**

We're just a couple of chefs working to create a place with real soul – where the food has personality, the surroundings are relaxed and the hospitality is warm and sincere", say Guy and Brittany Manning, chefs and owners of the thatched roofed Red Lion Freehouse. The is a modest description based on the reputation of this pub and its exceptional cuisine which has been awarded a Michelin star.

Troutbeck is their elegant 5 room guest house, close to the pub and situated on the banks of the River Avon with incredible views from the rooms' decks. The Red Lion offers simplicity in style which only enhances the focus on the food. Stripped wooden floors, a cosy wood burner and farmhouse style furniture keep the pub traditional in spirit. This is a winning combination for both locals and visitors alike.

ADDRESS

East Chisenbury, Pewsey
SN9 6AQ

PHONE

01980 671124

PUB GRUB
The Fish Pie

A mouthful of maritime delight, the
fish pie is a proudly rustic dish that is
as filling as it is flavoursome. Clouds of
buttery mashed potato and melted
cheddar top an unctuous filling of fish
and seafood, with smoked haddock,
salmon and prawns favourite
ingredients.

While the dish is now humbly
presented, its roots stem from a 900-
year-old royal tradition.

The Bull

DT6 3LF | DORSET | BRIDPORT

Just a few miles from Dorset's sought-after Jurassic Coast, the award-winning Bull Hotel has welcomed guests for centuries since its beginnings as a 16th-century coaching inn. The food is expertly prepared and beautifully presented, with something for everyone across its five menus.

Each of the 19 bedrooms is decorated in boutique hotel style with unique furnishings. For a real taste of grandeur, book a room with a four-poster bed and freestanding bathtub for an indulgent sleep and soak. Chesil Beach, Lyme Regis and the Golden Cap cliffs are all within a short drive.

ADDRESS

34 East St, Bridport
DT6 3LF

PHONE

01308 422878

The Swan

GL7 3NU | **GLOUCESTERSHIRE** | LECHLADE

The Swan Inn is a traditional 16th-century family-run pub in the peaceful market town of Lechlade. Situated on the edge of the picturesque Cotswolds, the pub is close to the River Thames where scenic boat tours can be taken, or you can walk the Thames Footpath.

The Swan feels like a locals pub with original stone interior walls and roaring fires. The menu here is traditional with pub classics available and homemade on the premises. Local ingredients are used where possible. This is a very dog-friendly pub, so the environment is relaxed and casual.

ADDRESS
Lechlade, Southrop, Gloucestershire
GL7 3NU

PHONE
01367 850205

Timbrell's Yard

BA15 1DE | WILTSHIRE | BRADFORD-ON-AVON

Timbrell's Yard is a stylish and contemporary riverside inn in the heart of Bradford-on-Avon. High ceilings, stripped wooden floors and an abundance of natural light from its large windows set the backdrop to the restaurant area which manages to cleverly fuse reclaimed furnishings with industrial lighting.

The award-winning food here is vibrant and delicious, thanks to executive chef Tom Blake, former head chef at River Cottage, who is obsessive about local, seasonal and authentic ingredients. Traceability is key and the menu proudly names their key suppliers. Rooms are beautifully furnished with elegant style.

ADDRESS

49 St Margaret's St, Bradford-on-Avon
BA15 1DE

PHONE

01225 869492

The Crabshell Inn

TQ7 1JZ | **DEVON** | KINGSBRIDGE

The Crabshell Inn has impressive views thanks to its enviable quayside position. You can watch estuary life from both inside and outside the restaurant. "Joyous, indulgent, freshly prepared fine food that loves to be enjoyed with friends and family," is the Crabshell Inn's philosophy.

With its waterside position, local seafood is the speciality. The pizzas are also locally renowned whilst their Zest Deli offers colourful Moroccan inspired salads for warmer days. Watch the sun shimmering on the water as boats bob up-and-down over a seafood board with a chilled glass of wine.

ADDRESS

The Quay, Embankment Rd,
Kingsbridge
TQ7 1JZ

PHONE

01548 852345

The Thatch

EX33 1LZ | **DEVON** | **BRAUNTON**

In the heart of Devon's surfing capital, The Thatch at Croyde, close to Braunton, is a lively pub inside a charmingly old 16th-century stone and thatch shell. Their menu tells the same story, featuring traditional pub classics alongside modern musts like burgers and nachos. There's plenty of seating out the front if you'd like to enjoy the sun, while the beamed, vaulted dining room offers a traditional space inside.

Saunton Sands, Putsborough Beach and Woolacombe Bay are all not far away and Croyde itself packs in plenty of coastal appeal. The Thatch offers bed and breakfast rooms to help you extend your stay in one of four enchanting historic properties in the village.

ADDRESS

14 Hobb's Hill, Croyde, Braunton
EX33 1LZ

PHONE

01271 890349

The Ferry Inn

TQ8 8ET | DEVON | SALCOMBE

Situated next to the harbour wall and overlooking the ombré blue water of picturesque Salcombe Harbour is The Ferry Inn. Owning one of the best positions in this beautiful region with its rolling hills and golden sands, the terrace, which sits parallel to the water, is one of the best spots for a drink in Salcombe.

The menu at The Ferry Inn is simple with burgers being a favourite. Classic dishes range from traditional fish and chips to lasagne. With its proximity to the water, seafood also features heavily on the menu. It is the exceptional views that people come here for. The pub itself is basic and unpretentious.

ADDRESS

Fore St, Salcombe
TQ8 8ET

PHONE

01548 844000

Ilfracombe

SOUTH WEST | PLACES WE LOVE |

This North Devon town has rejuvenated its image as an English seaside destination and home to the award-winning Landmark Theatre and Tunnels beaches. The scenic National Cycle Network Route to Woolacombe and The South West Coast Path from Minehead to Poole pass through Ilfracombe.

Salcombe

SOUTH WEST | PLACES WE LOVE |

Salcombe is one of Devon's most picturesque harbour towns, with views over the crystal clear water. Dolphins and a multitude of fishing boats call this scenic location home. Houses in an array of pastel tones form the backdrop, which sits close to the mouth of the sparkling Salcombe-Kingsbridge Estuary.

Dartmouth

SOUTH WEST | PLACES WE LOVE |

Dartmouth is set on the western bank of the estuary of the River Dart, which is a long narrow tidal river that runs inland as far as Totnes. Historic streets sit alongside the scenic river bank and combine to make this one of Devon's most attractive towns.

Boscastle

SOUTH WEST | PLACES WE LOVE |

The romantic and picturesque village of Boscastle on the north coast of Cornwall was once home to both busy fishing and stonemasonry trades. The village sits high above the harbour and is flanked by a breathtaking rugged and rocky coastline, making it the perfect creative inspiration for numerous artists and writers.

Portscatho

SOUTH WEST | PLACES WE LOVE |

Situated on the Roselands peninsula near to Truro on the edge of Gerrans Bay, Portscatho is a delightful part of Cornwall and a great area for walks around the harbour, the coastal path and the nearby beach. The steep slope down to the beach means that the views from the village itself are exceptional in all directions.

Polperro

SOUTH WEST | PLACES WE LOVE |

One of the most popular destinations in Cornwall, Polperro is a largely unspoiled fishing village on the southeast coast. The beach here is small and sandy and sports a fabulous little tidal pool ideal for first swimmers. Pretty cottages cling to the steep hillside of this quaint and picturesque harbour.

Mevagissey

SOUTH WEST | PLACES WE LOVE |

Mevagissey is an attractive village and fishing port five miles south of St. Austell. This was once the centre of Cornwall's pilchard fishery with boat building traditions dating back to 1745. The village still boasts a working harbour with local fishermen heading out each morning.

Weymouth

SOUTH WEST | PLACES WE LOVE |

Weymouth is a seaside town in Dorset located at the mouth of the River Wey. The Esplanade is composed of an attractive arc of terraces. Much of the architecture was constructed in the Georgian and Regency periods between 1770 and 1855 and commissioned by wealthy businessmen.

Glastonbury

SOUTH WEST | PLACES WE LOVE |

Glastonbury is a quaint town in Somerset known widely for the mammoth festival which takes place each year and also for its ancient and medieval sites, many of which are steeped in myth and legend. The Glastonbury Tor overlooks the town and is well worth the short walk to the summit where the surrounding fields are often shrouded in mist.

Wells

SOUTH WEST | PLACES WE LOVE |

Wells is often described as England's smallest city and is named after three wells dedicated to Saint Andrew, two of which are located within the grounds of the moated Bishop's Palace. The Cathedral is in the centre of the cobbled city while Wookey Hole Caves and Glastonbury are all a short drive away.

Castle Combe

SOUTH WEST | PLACES WE LOVE |

Castle Combe is often called Englands prettiest village and with good reason. Its a picture postcard village surrounded by beautiful countryside, perfect for walking. The thick stone walls and split stone tile roofs are typical of the Cotswolds and the By Brook and church add further charm to this very English village.

Dartmoor

SOUTH WEST | PLACES WE LOVE |

Dartmoor National Park is a large expanse of moorland in county Devon. Handsome Dartmoor ponies roam the often stark landscape, where craggy rocks, tors and wetlands cover the grounds. Neolithic tombs, ancient stone circles and abandoned farmhouses are also noteworthy places to visit.

Shaftsbury

Shaftesbury is an attractive market town in Dorset with a rich history dating back to Saxon times. The town's Gold Hill is one of the highlights with its stunning views over Blackmore Vale, steep cobbled street and stacked houses. The Mitre Pub enjoys these same excellent views from its outdoor deck and The Grosvenor Arms is another good option when seeking refreshment.

Padstow

Padstow is a charming working fishing port on the North Coast of Cornwall surrounded by stunning golden beaches. The town is a top foodie destination and is home to many of Rick Stein's great restaurants. A trip to Padstow is not complete without a spot of crabbing and a short boat trip over the Camel River to Rock.

Rock

On the eastern shore of the Camel Estuary, the village of Rock has a reputation as an upmarket holiday destination for the yachting set. The beach is a long stretch of golden sand which follows the estuary to the coast. The sand dunes behind mask the renowned and prestigious St Enodoc golf course.

Port Isaac

Port Isaac retains the essence of an historic fishing port, with its narrow winding streets, beautiful whitewashed quaint cottages and striking sandy working harbour. The series Doc Martin starring Martin Clunes is regularly filmed in the village which brings in some of the tourism as well as the glorious views, local galleries and arts and crafts shops.

South West England

CHAPTER FOUR

MIDLANDS

The Inn at Welland

WR13 6LN | **WORCESTERSHIRE** | WELLAND

The Inn at Welland offers magnificent views over the Malvern Hills. This award-winning pub and restaurant is nationally renowned with a menu focusing on fresh local produce, made from 'scratch' by a team with a vision and passion for quality food.

The stylish and contemporary interior features flagstone floors and walls in soft muted colours. When the weather is warm their terraced gardens offer the perfect English country setting. An external fireplace and cosy wool blankets enable you to enjoy alfresco drinks late into summer evenings or on cooler autumnal days.

ADDRESS
Hook Band, Welland
WR13 6LN

PHONE
01684 592317

The Littleton Arms

ST19 5AL | STAFFORDSHIRE | PENKRIDGE

The Littleton Arms, situated in the heart of Staffordshire, is an independently owned restaurant and pub with bedrooms. This 18th-century coaching inn has a reputation for excellent food, contemporary interiors and friendly staff. The menus are seasonal, designed by head chef Will Dean, using locally sourced ingredients from quality suppliers.

Traditional oak beams, fireplaces and wood-burners keep the pub cosy in the colder months. Food is served 7 days a week and is served from breakfast through to dinner with a vegan and kids' menu available. The menus are imaginative. Ten simple en-suite rooms continue the contemporary style of the pub and are available to guests.

ADDRESS

St.Michaels' Square, Penkridge
ST19 5AL

PHONE

01785 716300

The Fuzzy Duck

CV37 8DD | **WARWICKSHIRE** | ARMSCOTE

With a double aspect fireplace, this contemporary Cotswold pub is the perfect spot to enjoy a lazy weekend lunch or romantic supper with the ability to roll upstairs to one of their luxurious bedrooms, each named after a species of duck which can be found on the lakes of Armscote Manor.

Working with the best local suppliers to create delicious seasonal menus, the cuisine takes its lead from the beautiful surrounding Cotswolds and the abundant ingredients that can be found here. The pub itself feels luxurious and stylish with every detail considered. This is a Cotswold gem.

ADDRESS

Ilmington Road, Armscote
CV37 8DD

PHONE

01608 682635

The Bell

CV37 8NY | WARWICKSHIRE | STRATFORD-UPON-AVON

A former 18th-century coaching inn in the picturesque village of Alderminster, the gateway to the Cotswolds, The Bell has achieved an AA rosette status for its culinary excellence. Its seasonal menu harvests much of its produce from the local area and the Alscot Estate on which it sits.

The interior is stylish and vibrant with contemporary bedrooms featuring some of the inn's original beams and opulent furnishings. Views of the Stour Valley from the pub are stunning and the outside dining areas include a beautiful vine-covered decked terrace and lawned gardens.

ADDRESS

Alderminster, Stratford-up-on-Avon

CV37 8NY

PHONE

01789 450414

The Haughmond

SY4 4TZ | **SHROPSHIRE** | **SHREWSBURY**

The Haughmond is a modern coaching inn situated in the peaceful village of Upton Magna near Shrewsbury. The team here has a passion for fabulous food with local provenance and work these ingredients into their highly-regarded menus. The relaxing ambience, comfortable dining room and welcoming service are combined with beautiful views over the Wrekin hill.

Contemporary bedrooms are available on a bed and breakfast basis, each named after local deer, or in the case of their dog-friendly rooms, the resident (past and present) Staffordshire Bull Terriers; Basil and Boris. Award-winning breakfasts await you in the morning.

ADDRESS
Pelham Road, Shrewsbury
SY4 4TZ

PHONE
01743 709918

The Lion and Pheasant

SY1 1XJ | SHROPSHIRE | SHREWSBURY

Originally built in the 16th century, the Lion and Pheasant is a stylish house hotel in Shrewsbury with stunning views overlooking the River Severn and Shrewsbury Abbey. The elegant light muted interiors and textured details have a Scandinavian aesthetic, juxtaposed against the traditional original features from the oak beams to the roaring fires set within deep stone Inglenook fireplaces.

A beautifully maintained courtyard is perfect for enjoying evenings sampling wines from the Lion and Pheasant's comprehensive wine list and the delicious seasonal menu featuring local ingredients. Bedrooms are luxurious and individually styled and continue the stylish and contemporary design theme.

ADDRESS

49-50 Wyle Cop, Shrewsbury
SY1 1XJ

PHONE

01743 770345

The Duncombe Arms

DE6 2GZ | DERBYSHIRE | ASHBOURNE

The Duncombe Arms is an 1850s inn serving classic and modern British seasonal food of fine-dining quality in the warm, relaxed surroundings of a local country pub. Family owned, this eclectic and rustic pub features roaring fires, leather banquettes, polished wooden tables and candlelight to create a wonderful ambience.

The diverse wine menu features 98 wines, from value table wines to more refined selections, whilst the gin menu features 28 varieties. The garden offers a pretty place to enjoy summer barbecues under a shady umbrella. The picturesque garden cottage, just minutes from the pub and situated on the Wootton Hall Estate can be hired.

ADDRESS

Ellastone, Ashbourne
DE6 2GZ

PHONE

01335 324275

Guinness

The stout with staying power, the first batch of Guinness was produced in 1759. Incredibly, some of those early recipes continue to guide production today, with Guinness Original offering a taste of the 1821 beer on which it is based.

The brew is instantly recognisable with its velvety, dark colour and you can visit the brewery in Dublin for a roof-top pint.

The Nags Head

WR14 2JG | WORCESTERSHIRE | MALVERN

Quietly tucked at the foot of a hill in Malvern, take a pew at The Nags Head and enjoy booze with a view. The beer garden is rustic and lushly planted, while inside the free house features a traditional timber bar, eclectic furniture and vintage accessories. Within touching distance of the Malvern Hills, it's a wonderful Worcestershire watering hole.

Behind the bar, you'll be spoilt for choice with 24 whiskeys, 18 gins and a wine list combining old and new world bottles to peruse. There are also 15 ales on offer, three of which come from the pub's own St George's Brewery. Also on the menu are a range of daily specials, pub classics and global dishes, as well as a hearty Sunday roast.

ADDRESS

19-21 Bank Street, Malvern
WR14 2JG

PHONE

01684 574373

The Bell Inn

CV47 2BY | **WARWICKSHIRE** | **LADBROKE**

A hidden gem in Warwickshire, The Bell Inn in the picturesque village of Ladbroke lies on the popular Millennium Way walking trail, making it a popular pit-stop for hikers and locals alike. There's a pretty beer garden with plenty of outside seating, an atmospheric open fire and a cosy library to enjoy, so whether you're meeting for a casual drink or have something to celebrate, there's space to do it here.

The menu focuses on pub classics, ranging from traditional roasts to burgers, steak and fish, cooked with a refined twist. The pub is conveniently located for exploring the surrounding area, with the M40 only five miles distant and Warwick Castle reachable in under half an hour.

ADDRESS

Banbury Road, Ladbroke
CV47 2BY

PHONE

01926 811224

The Cow

DE6 5BE | DERBYSHIRE | DALBURY LEES

The Cow in Danbury Lees is a small 19th-century luxury boutique inn offering 12 new and beautifully decorated guest rooms and bathrooms. The casual dining restaurant and bar area have been stripped back to reveal the glorious heritage of the original building with its oak floors and beams, stone accents and fireplaces.

The Cow manages to successfully juxtapose contemporary furnishings against its original features. Interesting details include bar stools, which incorporate milk urns into the base, continuing The Cow theme. Bedrooms at The Cow are luxurious and exude style. The ever-changing à la carte menu utilises seasonal local produce alongside an extensive wine list.

ADDRESS

The Green, Dalbury Lees
DE6 5BE

PHONE

01332 824297

Hammer & Pincers

LE12 6ST | LEICESTERSHIRE, | LOUGHBOROUGH

Situated in the village of Wymeswold, Hammer and Pincers is considered to be one of the region's leading pubs for dining. Award-winning and respected by restaurant critics, the pub menu incorporates the finest local ingredients and everything is made from scratch in-house from the butter to the ice cream.

Seasonality is key to the menus and each dish is carefully considered and innovative. Unique flavours and imaginative combinations are concocted by owners Sandra and Danny Jimminson. Their past experience includes training at the Savoy hotel in London and work in Provence and St Moritz. The 10-course grazing menu is a popular choice.

ADDRESS

5 East Road, Wymeswold,
Loughborough
LE12 6ST

PHONE

01509 880735

Steamed Mussels

Often served simply to fill a deep bowl with their glistening inky shells, mussels make a hearty meal and are excellent when accompanied by a white wine or garlic sauce.

They are also great additions to a seafood chowder, although not all mussels are harvested from the sea – there are freshwater varieties, too. Blue mussels are England's most common variety.

The Olive Branch

LE15 7SH | NOTTINGHAMSHIRE | CLIPSHAM

The pub was originally three farm labourers' cottages which were knocked together to make a pub in 1890. Open fires, antique tables and chairs mixed with pine kitchen tables and benches create an informal atmosphere. Chestnuts are roasted on the fires in winter and homemade lemonade is served in the garden during summer.

The outside gardens and terrace are the perfect place to spend summer lunches or late evening dinners under the stars. The terrace also features a wood-fired pizza oven serving homemade pizzas topped with delicious local charcuterie, cheeses and herbs. Local vineyards and microbreweries contribute to the drinks menu.

ADDRESS

Main Street, Clipsham
LE15 7SH

PHONE

01780 410355

Brownlow Arms

NG32 2AZ | LINCOLNSHIRE | HOUGH ON THE HILL

The Brownlow Arms is an award-winning 17th-century country inn providing traditional values and hospitality combined with contemporary style. This pub provides a country house ambience with dark inky colours set against a beautiful backdrop of brick interior walls, oak panelling, wooden beams and open fires.

The comfy armchairs, in chic country fabrics, are perfect for snuggling into with a glass of red wine next to the fire on colder days. The atmospheric bar is made of geometric bricks and wood. The menus change with the seasons and feature imaginative and contemporary versions of classic British dishes.

ADDRESS

Grantham Road, Hough On The Hill

NG32 2AZ

PHONE

01400 250234

The Bustard Inn

NG34 8QG | **LINCOLNSHIRE** | SLEAFORD

The Bustard Inn is an award-winning, beautifully restored pub featuring original stone walls and timbers. Light airy interiors, solid wood tables and porcelain tiled floors create a relaxed and modern environment. French doors open on to a pretty courtyard. The cuisine uses British ingredients with international accents.

The solid oak bar, stone fireplace and flagstone, flooring create a characterful environment to enjoy one of their real ales which they are passionate about. Jazz musicians regularly play at The Bustard Inn much to the delight of guests.

ADDRESS

44 Main Street, South Rauceby, Sleaford
NG34 8QG

PHONE

01529 488250

The Woodhouse Arms

NG33 4NS | LINCOLNSHIRE | CORBY GLEN

The Woodhouse Arms offers modern dining in a beautifully converted pub, with large arched windows allowing floods of natural light, high beamed ceilings and rustic stone interior walls. wood-burners and open fires keep the pub cosy during the winter and during the summer months, guests spill outside to eat.

Bed and breakfast is are available in their three spacious, well-appointed rooms which follow the country luxe decor theme. The food is well presented and features dishes from classic rib eye steaks and fish and chips through to grilled halloumi and beetroot burgers.

ADDRESS

2 Bourne Road, Corby Glen
NG33 4NS

PHONE

01476 552452

Martin Arms

NG12 3FD | NOTTINGHAMSHIRE | COLSTON BASSETT

Situated in the village of Colton Bassett in the Vale of Belvoir, The Martin Arms is a traditional English pub with landscaped gardens overlooked by the village church. Dark reds, dark wood, open fire, candlelight and traditional pictures of Victorian life and hunting scenes decorate the walls and create the interior of this popular pub.

The menu is traditional with old English dishes such as duck faggots, huntsman pie and pork ribeye. Period furnishings enhance the old-world ambience. The pub has won numerous awards whilst the bar stocks a great range of ales and an extensive wine list.

ADDRESS

School Lane, Colston Bassett
NG12 3FD

PHONE

01949 81361

The White Horse

PE6 9PE | **LINCOLNSHIRE** | **BASTON**

The White Horse in Baston is an 18th-century country pub with a menu drawing from the finest seasonal and local produce, prepared by head chef Ben Clark. Popular pub classics are served alongside internationally influenced dishes, all incorporating the best of the what the season has to offer.

The White horse is owned by the Field family who transformed both the interior and exterior of the pub by incorporating materials from their own farm such as the Sycamore Tree trunk in the snug bar. The pub has a wood burner and candles lit for colder days and an outside terrace which is perfect for summer lunches.

ADDRESS
4 Church Street, Baston
PE6 9PE

PHONE
01778 560923

The Bull & Swan

PE9 2LJ | LINCOLNSHIRE | STAMFORD

The Bull and Swan is a 16th-century honey-stone pub in beautiful Stamford. The pub recently turned its courtyard into an abundant kitchen garden, with ranks of raised beds all planted up with herbs, vegetables and fruit trees. The pizza potting shed is another draw to the garden which between April and September hosts an outdoor cinema.

The interior has a country house ambience. Painted in popular inky hues with dark wood furniture, portraiture on the walls and chocolate leather seating, wood-burners and fires warm the pub. Luxurious bedrooms with quirky details are available to guests.

ADDRESS

24 High St, Street Martins,
Stamford
PE9 2LJ

PHONE

01780 766412

The High Field

B15 3DP | **WEST MIDLANDS** | **BIRMINGHAM**

Forget everything you think you know about pubs at The High Field in Edgbaston, because there's no country idyll here. Instead, a staggeringly modern Art Deco building welcomes you inside, where luxe furniture, Scandi-style accessories and expanses of glazing give the wood-panelled walls a distinctly modern identity. A chic city oasis, there's also a terrace and garden to explore so that you can enjoy draught beer alfresco.

The same level of luxury applies to the menu: steaks are dry aged for 28 days and brasserie-style dishes inject an exciting menu twist. Ideal for celebrations, you can book a private dining room and spend the night in one of 12 boutique bedrooms in the pub's Victorian villa next door.

ADDRESS

22 Highfield Rd, Birmingham
B15 3DP

PHONE

0121 227 7068

Lincoln

MIDLANDS | PLACES WE LOVE |

Lincoln is a beautiful medieval cathedral city in the West Midlands, with over 2000 years of history as a town. As well as the Cathedral, there's a fantastic castle, excellent shopping, quirky tearooms and a good choice of fine dining. We suggest a walk up the rightly named steep hill followed by a visit to The Collection galleries.

Shrewsbury

MIDLANDS | PLACES WE LOVE |

Shrewsbury is a traditional market town filled with medieval architecture, it lies within a giant loop of the River Severn and is renowned for its castle, spires, abbey, parklands and half-timbered houses. Higgledy-piggledy streets and lanes are plentiful and very characteristic, some of which have bizarre names such as Dogpole and Mardol.

Stamford

MIDLANDS | PLACES WE LOVE |

Stamford is widely renowned as one of the finest stone towns in England. Cobbled streets, five medieval churches, the beautiful River Welland and a plethora of narrow alleyways are all good reasons to visit. On top of that, the bustling Friday Market overwhelms the town with eager shoppers and great stalls selling local veg, meats, pies, bread and fresh fish.

The Peak District

MIDLANDS | PLACES WE LOVE |

The Peak District offers breathtaking views and endless possibilities for walking, cycling and wildlife watching. Steep limestone valleys, moorland and caves are in abundance. Founded in 1951, the Peak District was England's first National Park and is Europe's busiest.

Our App makes it easy to find a great pub nearby

If you like our Pub Guide, you will love our app. Hundreds of recommendations in your pocket. Helpfully organised by which one is nearest to your location.

Available for iOS and Android.

Download now from
bestofengland.com/app

The Midlands

Cromer

A148

Holt

A140

A1065

A15

134

A47

A140

A16

A16

A47

Norwich

A10

A1(M)

Peterborough

Great Yarmo

A11

A140

A1065

A140

A12 Southwold

A11

Cambridge

A1 Aldeburgh

A131

A1(M) A10

M11

A12

Ipswich

Clacton-on-Sea

M25 A12

M1 M11

A46

A158

A16

CHAPTER FIVE

THE EAST

The Ramsholt Arms

IP12 3AB | SUFFOLK | RAMSHOLT

A popular riverside pub, situated on the scenic banks of the river Deben. The pub is located down a country lane and is a relaxing spot if you are looking to get away from the hustle and bustle. Dishes include favourites such as fish pie and slow cooked beef stew.

Taken over by the owners of the nearby Ufford Crown, the pub was given a complete refurbishment in 2013. There is a small stretch of beach on which to let the kids run free and from where locals launch their boats. On a sunny afternoon, there are few places we would rather be. Dogs are welcome.

ADDRESS

Dock Road, Ramsholt
IP12 3AB

PHONE

01394 411209

The Brisley Bell Inn

NR20 5DW | NORFOLK | BRISLEY

The Brisley Bell Inn is a 17th-century pub which has been tastefully and sympathetically renovated to become a stunning destination pub. In addition to the bar area, there is a quiet dining room and a cosy snug kitted out with books and an open fire.

There is also a bright and spacious garden room for al fresco dining in summer which doubles up as a live music space. Food is reasonably priced and best to book ahead as it can get very busy. Guest beers are rotated each month & dogs are welcome.

ADDRESS
The Green, Brisley
NR20 5DW

PHONE
01362 668040

The Gunton Arms

NR11 8TZ | NORFOLK | THORPE MARKET

The Gunton Arms is a unique pub located within a historic 1,000-acre deer park dating back to the 18th-century. Art dealer, Ivor Braka bought the pub in 2009 and spent 2 years renovating which included selecting appropriate pieces from his art collection with works by Tracey Emin and Damien Hirst now hung on the walls.

The menu is curated by Mark Hix and includes venison caught from within the grounds. Brancaster mussels and Cromer crab are popular with the walkers who frequent the pub. Roaring fires feature throughout, dogs are welcome and a private dining room is available.

ADDRESS
Cromer Road, Thorpe Market
NR11 8TZ

PHONE
01263 832010

The Kings Head

NR25 7AR | NORFOLK | LETHERINGSETT

The Kings Head in Letheringsett is nestled just outside the bustling Norfolk town of Holt. Housed within a handsome Georgian Manor from 1808 that has no less than three fires to create the bona fide country pub atmosphere. Ceilings are vaulted, shelves are adorned with books and grandfather clocks chime in the background. All of these details combine to create a homely welcome.

Quality ale is a priority with at least three available when we visited. There is also a large country garden with a willow maze and climbing tower to keep the children amused. Dogs are welcome.

ADDRESS

Holt Road, Letheringsett
NR25 7AR

PHONE

01263 712691

The Lifeboat Inn

PE36 6LT | NORFOLK | THORNHAM

The Lifeboat Inn is a 16th-century inn located on a beautiful section of the North Norfolk Coast. The pub is tucked away down a quiet country lane and so provides a welcome respite from the hustle and bustle. You will certainly be glad you made the trip once you have sampled their fish pie, so popular that they were asked to share the recipe in their local magazine.

The interior has been tastefully refurbished while being respectful of the original features such as wooden beams and a large open fireplace. Dog-friendly and ideal for bird watchers being located on the edge of the Holme Dunes National Nature Reserve.

ADDRESS

Ship Lane, Thornham
PE36 6LT

PHONE

01485 512236

PUB GRUB
Raw Oysters

Head to the South East to sample
some of England's finest oysters in
season. Heralded as the ultimate
seafood treat, the process of eating one
is far from elegant as you lift the oyster
– shell and all – and gulp the contents
down.

Despite being so distinctive, raw
oysters pair well with a surprising
range of flavours, from tangy lemon to
ginger and peppers.

The Plough

MK44 2EX | BEDFORDSHIRE | BOLNHURST

The Plough in Bolnhurst is situated in a 15th-century Medieval building which has been meticulously refurbished. This is an independent pub which is proud of its food and its ability to choose its favourite local producers to supply its seasonal menu.

Leather armchairs, wooden tables, roaring log fires, candles and lots of thoughtful details fill the interior of the pub. Picnic rugs are provided for the garden, which offers great al fresco dining opportunities.

ADDRESS
Kimbolton Road, Bolnhurst
MK44 2EX

PHONE
01234 376274

The White Pheasant

CB7 5LQ | CAMBRIDGESHIRE | ELY

Country dining is quite an experience at The White Pheasant in Ely. With a cosy open fire, stripped wooden floors and culinary excellence, the emphasis is on seasonal, locally sourced produce alongside award-winning wines. This is a family owned restaurant with a regional reputation.

The presentation and quality of food are exceptional and brought to you by Head Chef Calvin Holland, who has previously cooked at some of the UK's finest and Michelin Starred restaurants. The interior is minimal and contemporary with wooden tables and lots of natural light.

ADDRESS
21 Market St, Fordham, Ely
CB7 5LQ

PHONE
01638 720414

The Flitch of Bacon

CM6 3HT | ESSEX | DUNMOW

Tim Allen's The Flitch of Bacon Inn supports farmers and artisan producers by combining local produce with the very best European larder, to create dishes celebrating traditional British cooking, with a contemporary twist. It is all about the food here and is brought to you lovingly by Allen, who was previously the head chef at the then Michelin starred Wild Rabbit.

The restaurant is very minimal with leather banquettes and simple modern furnishings. The external terrace area has a vintage Citroen van which doubles as a summer cocktail bar and sits perfectly next to the outdoor kitchen.

ADDRESS

The Street, Little Dunmow
CM6 3HT

PHONE

01371 821660

The Rose and Crown

PE31 7LX | NORFOLK | SNETTISHAM

Dating back to the 14th-century, The Rose and Crown in the village of Snettisham is a hidden gem with plenty of old-world character; from the low ceilings with their ancient beams to the pamment floors and roaring log fires. The menu makes use of the local ingredients from the mussels, oysters and samphire to the fresh herbs and local game.

Built to house the builders working on the nearby St.Mary's church, this little white stone pub, embellished with colourful cascading roses, has been the focal point of village life for over 700 years. The walled garden is a pretty spot to enjoy a chilled glass of wine.

ADDRESS

Old Church Road, Snettisham
PE31 7LX

PHONE

01485 541382

The Fox at Willian

SG6 2AE | **HERTFORDSHIRE** | LETCHWORTH GARDEN CITY

The Fox at Willian is a stylish and award-winning country pub and fine dining restaurant in the scenic village of Willian. With contemporary country interiors, The Fox overlooks the village pond, surrounded by weeping willows. The pub garden spills onto the village green for outside drinking on summer days.

Locally sourced, seasonal ingredients are key to the delicious and considered menu and they serve their own Brancaster Brewery brews alongside regularly changing guest ales. The Fox at Willian offers 8 bespoke country-smart bedrooms which are all well-appointed and luxurious in style.

ADDRESS

1870 Willian Rd, Letchworth Garden City
SG6 2AE

PHONE

01462 480233

The Chequers Inn

PE36 6LY | NORFOLK | THORNHAM

The Chequers Inn in Thornham is a traditional, 16th-century pub with low beamed ceilings and a large open fireplace. This beautifully renovated former coaching inn on the North Norfolk coast offers daily specials in their contemporary dining room or out in the courtyard are two unique cedar wood pavilions, both perfect for a spot of al fresco dining.

The pub is an ideal stop off as part of a day out at RSPB Titchwell Marsh which is less than a mile away or when visiting Brancaster and Holkham beaches, both of which are a short drive away. Dog-friendly.

ADDRESS

High Street, Thornham
PE36 6LY

PHONE

01485 512229

The White Horse

PE31 8BY | **NORFOLK** | BRANCASTER STAITHE

Overlooking some of North Norfolk's finest marshland and beyond to the sea is the stylish White Horse in Brancaster Staithe. Lobster pots and oyster beds can be seen from the light and airy restaurant. Here you can sample some of Norfolk's freshest seafood in their award-winning restaurant.

The White Horse is popular given the ideal location from which to explore this area of outstanding natural beauty. Their conservatory makes lunch with a view on a sunny afternoon or dinner on a stormy night equally enjoyable.

ADDRESS
Main Road, Brancaster Staithe
PE31 8BY

PHONE
01485 210262

The Duck Inn

PE31 8QD | NORFOLK | STANHOE

The Duck Inn is an award-winning pub with a stripped back elegance, allowing the culinary talent to take centre stage. The ambience here is relaxed and sophisticated. Fresh flowers and candlelit tables sit against a backdrop of characterful brick walls and warming fires.

The kitchen is run by Ben Handley whose culinary highlights include Brancaster crab, Scotch quail eggs and Norfolk steamed mussels. Local sourcing of their ingredients is important with their meat supplied by nearby Holkham Estate and herbs sourced from their own garden.

ADDRESS

Burnham Road, Stanhoe

PE31 8QD

PHONE

01485 518330

The Ingham Swan

NR12 9AB | NORFOLK | INGHAM

The Ingham Swan is an award-winning, 14th-century coaching inn located within this pretty Norfolk hamlet to the North East of Norwich. The menu "strikes a balance between heritage and inventive cuisine" with dishes including chorizo roast sea bream and pan roast monkfish noisette.

The owners maintain land on a local farm where the majority of the restaurant's seasonal British produce is grown. Oak floors and inglenook fireplaces ensure the traditional feel of this inn has been maintained. There are also 4 rustic bedrooms situated in the former stables.

ADDRESS

Sea Palling Road, Ingham
NR12 9AB

PHONE

01692 581099

The Westleton Crown

IP17 3AD | **SUFFOLK** | WESTLETON

The Westleton Crown is a 12th-century coaching inn on the Suffolk Heritage coast. Situated within the picturesque village of Westleton, this pub has been serving the locals for over 800 years. There is a traditional bar area but also a large and bright dining room to the rear which opens up onto a courtyard garden.

Local farmers provide their meat and the fish is brought in daily from the boats in Lowestoft. Dunwich beach is two miles from here and Southwold and Aldeburgh are not far. Dogs are welcome. Prince William and the Duchess of Cambridge recently stayed when attending a friend's wedding in the area.

ADDRESS

The Street, Westleton
IP17 3AD

PHONE

01728 648777

The Pork Pie

The classic pork pie originates from the characterful Leicestershire town of Melton Mowbray – amble along the shopping streets to enjoy the smell of pork pies cooking wafting from bakeries.

The dish itself is deliciously simple, made from hot water crust pastry, jelly and pork. Luxury takes on this cold pie often include hard-boiled egg centres or game meat.

Galvin Green Man

CM3 1BG | ESSEX | GREAT WALTHAM

The Galvin Green Man is said to be one of the oldest pubs in Essex, built in 1341. Today roaring fires and the timber-framed bar are beautiful reminders of the pub's historic past. The pub is a return home for Michelin starred Essex-born brothers, Chris & Jeff Galvin.

The River Chelmer runs through the scenic pub garden at the Galvin Green Man. As an addition to the pub, The Galvin Brothers have added a sophisticated and contemporary restaurant in an impressive building with a centralised wood burner and panoramic views. The menu focuses on refined British cuisine, with carefully sourced seasonal ingredients.

ADDRESS

Main Road, Howe Street, Great Waltham
CM3 1BG

PHONE

01245 408 820

The Ship at Dunwich

IP17 3DT | **SUFFOLK** | DUNWICH

The Ship is located in the quiet, seaside village of Dunwich within walking distance of the long, shingle beach and a short drive from Aldeburgh and Southwold. This once thriving medieval port is now a quiet retreat being surrounded by nature reserves and monastic ruins.

Inside, a fire is kept roaring in winter to warm the ramblers and dog walkers who flock to this rugged area of East Anglia. There is a large garden to the rear to savour a well earned afternoon drink in the warmer months of the year. Ideal for walkers looking to explore this beautiful stretch of English coastline. Dog-friendly.

ADDRESS
St. James. Street, Dunwich
IP17 3DT

PHONE
01728 648219

The George

CO10 8BA | SUFFOLK | CAVENDISH

The George is a charming 16th-century gastro pub situated on the edge of the village green of Cavendish within the Stour Valley. Cavendish is one of the prettiest villages in Suffolk with period thatched cottages, antique shops and a medieval church.

This historic pub has a simple yet tasteful interior and a small, shaded courtyard garden. Classics include cheese ploughmans, the house burger and freshly caught oysters. There are five guest bedrooms available for bed and breakfast. Dogs are welcome.

ADDRESS

The Green, Cavendish
CO10 8BA

PHONE

01787 280248

The Queen

IP13 7AD | **SUFFOLK** | **BRANDESTON**

The Queen focuses on locally produced, beautifully cooked food. With their own kitchen garden harvesting an abundant array of vegetables and herbs throughout the year, the menu showcases these ingredients alongside other pub classics, always featuring the best local ingredients.

This is a family business and the pub projects the ambience and aesthetic of a farmhouse with lots of carefully considered details, cosy fires and fresh flowers in milk bottles highlighting the tables. Behind the kitchen garden is an area for glamping in shepherds' huts filled with luxurious little touches.

ADDRESS
The Street, Brandeston
IP13 7AD

PHONE
01728 685307

Long Melford Swan

CO10 9JQ | SUFFOLK | LONG MELFORD

The Swan is a two AA rosette restaurant in the heart of Long Melford, a delightful Suffolk village less than two hours from London. The menu is modern English cuisine with dishes including dry-aged beef Wellington, skate wing with cockles and steak & kidney pudding.

The dining space is contemporary and sophisticated and has been extended with a bright garden room. There are also seven boutique bedrooms should you wish to spend the night. Dogs and well-behaved children are welcome in the bar area. The Duck Deli is the latest addition to the building and is located next door.

ADDRESS

Hall Street, Long Melford
CO10 9JQ

PHONE

01787 464545

The White Horse Inn

IP13 8JR | SUFFOLK | BADINGHAM

The White Horse at Badingham is a picturesque 15th-century coaching inn with wisteria creeping up the walls and a beautiful outdoor area for enjoying their summer pizza oven. Interesting details inside include original open fires and exposed beams.

The pub is often candlelit, adding to the cosy ambience. Their real ales come from a number of local independent breweries and Giggler, a traditional local cider, is sourced from Bramfield only 8 miles away.

ADDRESS
Low St, Badingham
IP13 8JR

PHONE
01728 638280

The Orange Tree

PE36 6LY | NORFOLK | THORNHAM

Vibrant roses climb up the 400-year-old white stone walls of The Orange Tree, creating an idyllic approach as you arrive. The area is perfect for walks on the nearby sweeping sandy beaches and peaceful harbour where working fishing boats still bring in the daily catch.

The Orange Tree is a contemporary, award-winning pub in one of Norfolk's most picturesque regions. The innovative menu focuses on its access to some of the finest seafood the country has to offer.

ADDRESS

High St, Thornham, Hunstanton
PE36 6LY

PHONE

01485 512213

The Victoria Inn

NR23 1RG | NORFOLK | HOLKHAM

Fresh, local and seasonal produce is the focus of the cuisine at The Victoria in Holkham. The quality of their ingredients is paramount, from the shellfish, fish or samphire from the north Norfolk coast to the beef from their farms on the Holkham Estate.

Close to the golden sands of Holkham Beach and at the gates of the family's Palladian ancestral home, Holkham Hall, The Victoria is well positioned to explore the best of the region's villages and atmospheric beaches. Rooms are available and mix antique furnishings with modern comfort.

ADDRESS
Park Rd, Holkham, Wells-next-the-Sea
NR23 1RG

PHONE
01328 711008

The Crown and Castle

IP12 2LJ | **SUFFOLK** | ORFORD

The Crown and Castle is situated in the pretty village of Orford, on the banks of the river Ore and close to the town of Aldeburgh. With a multitude of local artisanal food producers, the restaurant places a high emphasis on food provenance and devotes much time to the art of sourcing the finest local and seasonal ingredients.

The Terrace restaurant, open in the summer months, offers views of the 12th-century, Orford Castle. The restaurant is light and modern in style with upholstered banquettes and dark wooden floors. The dishes are unpretentious yet inventive. Comfortable and contemporary rooms are available to guests.

Orford, Woodbridge
IP12 2LJ

PHONE

01394 450205

Cambridge

EAST OF ENGLAND | PLACES WE LOVE |

Cambridge is an impressive university city and an architectural delight, with spires jutting along the skyline in every direction. It's home to many beautiful museums and art galleries, independent shops and has an excellent culinary scene. The river Cam is a wonderful way to explore the city via a classic punting boat.

Aldeburgh

EAST OF ENGLAND | PLACES WE LOVE |

Aldeburgh is a traditional seaside town with plenty to offer the visiting tourist. A pebble beach runs from the Martello Tower overlooking the harbour at the south of town to the controversial Scallop sculpture in the North.

Burnham Market

EAST OF ENGLAND | PLACES WE LOVE |

Burnham Market is arguably the prettiest village in North Norfolk, with its traditional feel, a busy butchers, fishmongers, post office and chemist. Along with some handy shops to pick up the necessaries, there are some great places to stop for food and drink.

Wells-next-the-Sea Beach

EAST OF ENGLAND | PLACES WE LOVE |

Wells Beach is easily one of Norfolk's finest. The sand goes on for miles and miles and hundreds of quirky colourful beach huts on stilts run along the pine forest wall and back dunes. You can access the beach via the nearby carpark or it's a short walk or miniature rail ride from the town along the East Fleet river.

Woodbridge

Woodbridge is only eight miles from the coast and a similar distance from Ipswich, yet it is often overlooked. This pretty, historic market town is filled with treats for those visiting; highlights include the Tide Mill, Yacht Harbour and St Mary's.

Blakeney

Blakeney is one of Norfolk's most enchanting coastal villages and makes an ideal base from which to explore the North Norfolk coast. Boats leave the harbour daily to observe the seals who live on Blakeney Point and there is an enjoyable walk to the remote lifeboat station there.

Bury St. Edmunds

Bury St. Edmunds is an historic market town in Suffolk. Attractive medieval architecture is apparent throughout and elegant buildings such as the grand Cathedral and Abbey Gardens are a free treat to visitors and locals. Other attractions include the Greene King Brewery, the Theatre Royal and the Apex music venue.

Bawdsey Village

Located on the other side of the river Deben from Felixstowe is the handsome village of Bawdsey. A scattering of houses, a shingly sandy river beach and a handful of boats. The calm waters are great for skimming a few stones and paddling.

Lavenham

EAST OF ENGLAND | PLACES WE LOVE |

Half-timbered houses and higgledy-piggledy storefronts are in plentitude in Lavenham. Take a walk around this beautiful village and try and spot the prettiest building. They're coated in a mix of mid-toned pastels from Suffolk pink to burnt orange and light up the village like an artist's palette.

Cavendish

EAST OF ENGLAND | PLACES WE LOVE |

Cavendish in Suffolk is a picture postcard village nestled in the Stour Valley, famous for its thatched cottages and quaint, rambling village green.

Walberswick

EAST OF ENGLAND | PLACES WE LOVE |

Walberswick is an attractive, secluded coastal village with much traditional charm. Main attractions include the nearby harbour with a spot of crabbing and a walk along the river Blyth and of course, the unspoiled sand dunes and beach are a must.

Ely

EAST OF ENGLAND | PLACES WE LOVE |

Thousands of visitors from all over the world flock to Ely each year to gaze in wonder at this magnificent Cathedral. Lovers of architecture can admire the ornate stonework and intricate details, while historians can delve deep into its foundations, back to AD 672 when St Etheldreda built an Abbey Church on the site.

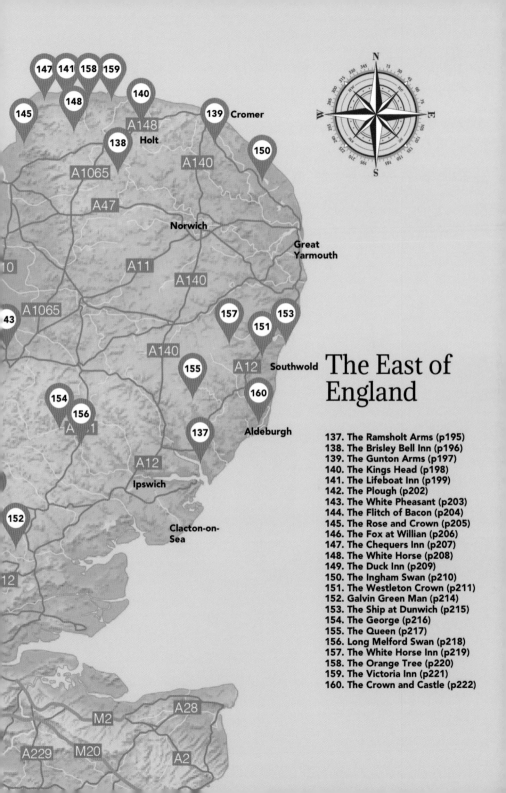

The East of England

N
NW NE
W E
SW SE
S

147 141 158 159
148
145
140
A148
139 Cromer
138 Holt
150
A140
A1065
A47
Norwich
A11
Great Yarmouth
A1065
A140
157 153
151
A140
155 A12 Southwold
160
154
156
A11
137 Aldeburgh
A12
Ipswich
152
Clacton-on-Sea
12
M2 A28
A229 M20 A2

The Drunken Duck

LA22 0NG | CUMBRIA | AMBLESIDE

The Drunken Duck is located near Ambleside. Offering mesmerising views towards Windermere from its garden and terrace, the interior offers rustic country style with soft greens contrasting against chocolate leather armchairs, stripped oak floors and vintage artwork. With their own micro-brewery, the local ales and beers have a major appeal with locals and visitors.

The menu at the Drunken Duck is imaginative with interesting and contemporary combinations created by the open kitchen. The roaring fire warms customers up after blustery walks. The pub offers bedrooms decorated in a country luxe style.

ADDRESS

Barngates, Ambleside
LA22 0NG

PHONE

015394 36347

The Cholmondeley Arms

SY14 8HN | CHESHIRE | MALPAS

In the heart of the Cheshire countryside, adjacent to Cholmondeley Castle and within a former Victorian village schoolhouse, is the Cholmondeley Arms. The pub has earned a reputation for its freshly cooked, locally sourced food from artisan bakers, farmers, butchers, fishermen and cheesemakers.

The pub interior is magnificent and characterful with high ceilings, brick interior walls, open fires and enormous windows. The carved oak bar hosts an incredibly lengthy and diverse array of gins. Luxuriously comfortable rooms are available over the road at The Headmaster's House.

ADDRESS

Wrenbury Road, Malpas
SY14 8HN

PHONE

01829 720300

The Roebuck Inn

WA16 7HX | CHESHIRE | MOBBERLEY

The Roebuck is an award-winning inn in the village of Mobberley dating back to 1708. The interior of rich burgundy banquettes, cabinets full of wine bottles and glasses, brass mirrors, dark woods and candlelight create a cosy ambience. The restaurant is more bistro than pub and the quirky decor gives the inn an air of eccentricity.

The menu offers sharing boards and plenty of globally inspired dishes alongside their famous stone-baked pizzas. Bedrooms here are atmospheric and luxurious. Painted in dark rich colours, the rooms are decorated with roll top baths, opulent fabrics, chandeliers, oversized freestanding mirrors and exposed brick walls. Faded grandeur reflects the theme.

ADDRESS

Mill Lane, Mobberley
WA16 7HX

PHONE

01565 873939

The Fishpool Inn

CW8 2HP | CHESHIRE | DELAMERE

The Fishpool Inn in Delamere, Cheshire is a newly and sympathetically renovated sandstone gastro inn dating back to the 18th century. The innovative open kitchen prepares traditional and modern British and European dishes using only the finest locally sourced seasonal ingredients.

The interior of The Fishpool Inn reflects the cultural heritage of Cheshire, with references to its equestrian and country estate links. Artwork of country scenes and horses deck the walls. Traditional wooden beams and roaring fires are mixed with more contemporary details such as industrial pendant lighting and vaulted ceilings.

ADDRESS
Fishpool Road, Delamere
CW8 2HP

PHONE
01606 883277

Tan Hill Inn

DL11 6ED | **YORKSHIRE** | RICHMOND

Tan Hill Inn is situated in Swaledale in an isolated position in the Yorkshire Dales. This historic inn dates back to the 17th century with its flag-stone floor, exposed beams and welcoming fire. Tan Hill Inn holds the title of Britain's highest public house at 1,732 feet (528m) above sea level.

Tan Hill is an unpretentious, traditional pub with magnificent views over the dales. It has become a bit of an institution and the music events here have been legendary including when The Arctic Monkeys once performed here. The food is traditional and they proudly host many of the local breweries.

ADDRESS
Long Causeway, Richmond
DL11 6ED

PHONE
01833 628246

The Black Swan

CA17 4NQ | **YORKSHIRE** | RAVENSTONEDALE

Situated in the conservation village of Ravenstonedale in the Eden Valley below the Howgill Fells, The Black Swan focuses on a local Cumbrian menu using the seasons to inspire the locally available ingredients. The provenance of the food is key and they openly list the artisanal suppliers of their ingredients, from the dairy and bakery to the fishermen.

With a riverside garden open in the warmer months, The Black Swan offers a homely environment with wood-burners and a relaxed atmosphere. Head chef Scott Fairweather leads a passionate team who place a strong emphasis on food presentation.

ADDRESS

Ravenstonedale, Kirkby
Stephen
CA17 4NQ

PHONE

The Inn at Whitewell

BB7 3AT | LANCASHIRE | CLITHEROE

Sitting high on the banks of the River Hodder, The Inn at Whitewell began life in the 1300s as a small manor house, lived in by the keepers of the Royal forest. During the 1700s, the building began its life as an inn. The food ethos focuses on "using only the best local ingredients, cooked simply to let the real quality shine through."

The inn's interior is traditional with elegantly designed rooms, roaring fires and incredible views over the breathtaking countryside. Wooden tables and chairs sit on flagstone floors and the walls are adorned with equestrian artwork.

ADDRESS
Forest of Bowland, Clitheroe
BB7 3AT

PHONE
01200 448222

PUB GRUB
Sausage & Mash

England has a proud history of butchery and you'll find many independent merchants present on high streets nationwide to this day. A plate of sausages and buttery mashed potatoes is the perfect way to taste the tradition.

As butchers increasingly value heritage breeds, the dish receives a flavour twist, with venison or rare breed meat flavouring the sausage.

Freemasons at Wiswell

BB7 9DF | LANCASHIRE | WISWELL

The Freemasons at Wiswell is considered one of the best pubs in the country and is renowned for its impressive cuisine created by chef-proprietor Steven Smith. Nestled in the Ribble Valley, this country pub cleverly mixes a refined traditional experience with contemporary flair. The food is sophisticated and the ambience is homely.

The hunting lodge theme runs throughout and is evidenced in the decor; with equestrian and hunting illustrations, deer and other taxidermy heads embellishing the walls. For those wanting to sample chef-patron Steven Smith's innovative culinary style, the Tasting Menu is a must.

ADDRESS

8 Vicarage Fold, Wiswell
BB7 9DF

PHONE

01254 822218

The Red Pump

BB7 3DA | LANCASHIRE | CLITHEROE

With its origins dating back to 1756, The Red Pump Inn is an elegant rural country pub with rooms. The recently restored inn is quickly gaining a reputation as a fine steak restaurant. Stone flag floors, oak beams and cosy fires style the interior. The inn is proudly supplied by the famous Ginger Pig of London.

A good selection of international wines, often selected from quality, lesser known vineyards feature on the wine list. The meat selected by The Red Pump Inn is from cattle which have matured slowly, having grazed on a natural diet of grass and hay. The dishes are simple and cooked with passion.

ADDRESS

Clitheroe Road, Bashall Eaves,
Clitheroe
BB7 3DA

PHONE

01254 826227

The General Tarleton Inn

HG5 0PZ | **YORKSHIRE** | KNARESBOROUGH

Award-winning food is served at The General Tarleton Inn, close to the beautiful spa town of Harrogate. Proud of the provenance of their ingredients, dishes are innovative and strive to achieve the best of the local and seasonal produce available. The 18th-century inn has been decorated in a contemporary style with cosy touches from the vibrant velvet chesterfields to the wood burner.

The Yorkshire stone interior walls are a nod to the inn's heritage and the lighting and candlelight enhance the atmosphere. Their luxurious bedrooms are individually themed but all with comfort at the forefront.

ADDRESS

Ferrensby, Knaresborough
HG5 0PZ

PHONE

01423 340284

Assheton Arms

BB7 4BJ | **LANCASHIRE** | **DOWN**

Multi-award winning Assheton Arms is a Grade II listed pub in the conservation village of Downham. With a great atmosphere in the evening, their chefs use only the finest ingredients, with fish sourced by Chris Neve (Fleetwood coast), meat from Roaming Roosters and vegetables from Lady Clitheroe's garden.

Renowned for its stunning views across the Ribble Valley, Downham has been a popular TV and film location since the 1960's with productions including Whistle Down the Wind filmed in the village. A recent refurbishment of the pub offers stylish and luxurious accommodation.

ADDRESS
Top Row, Down
BB7 4BJ

PHONE
01200 441227

Hare and Hounds

LA8 8PN | CUMBRIA | LEVENS

The Hare and Hounds is situated in a perfect position for visiting the Lake District and is a fully refurbished coaching inn dating back to the 17th century. They provide great home-inspired meals, using local ingredients where possible. The black slate floors and open fire create a cosy and convivial atmosphere.

Much like the styling of the pub and restaurant below, the comfy rooms are a fusion of Victorian and contemporary in design. The Hare and Hounds is nestled in stunning surroundings and is a welcome place to rejuvenate after a day of walking or being outdoors.

ADDRESS
Church Road, Levens
LA8 8PN

PHONE
015395 60004

The Pheasant

CA13 9YE | CUMBRIA | COCKERMOUTH

The Pheasant in Bassenthwaite is stylistically stuck in a bit of a time warp but the quality of food and service remains popular today. Using a number of local ingredients in their dishes, you can choose to eat in the slightly more formal Fell Restaurant or the relaxed Bistro or bar.

Surrounded by the beautiful scenery of Lake Bassenthwaite, this 17th-century coaching inn is a good stop off for walkers and dogs are also welcomed. The pub garden offers limited seating but a pretty environment to have a drink on warmer days. The characterful and traditional bar area is a cosy place to sit with a glass of wine.

ADDRESS

Bassenthwaite Lake, Cockermouth
CA13 9YE

PHONE

017687 76234

The Plough

LA6 1PJ | CUMBRIA | COW BROW

The Plough Inn near Kirkby Lonsdale is a tastefully styled, contemporary restaurant and hotel situated inside a characterful old coaching inn. With beautiful original beams set against freshly painted walls and a neutral colour palette, the quality and attention to detail offer a little luxury in the countryside.

Roaring wood-burners add to the relaxing ambience at The Plough and the menu offers quality British cuisine, with the meat and other specific ingredients sourced locally. The bedrooms offer superb accommodation with large bathrooms, roll top baths and some luxurious furnishings.

ADDRESS
Lupton, Cow Brow
LA6 1PJ

PHONE
015395 67700

Fenwick Arms

LA2 9LA | **LANCASHIRE** | CATON

The beautiful Fenwick Arms is over 250 years old and exudes historic and atmospheric charm. The stylish interior cleverly incorporates the beautiful features of the old building, with its stone walls, large open fires and oak floors into a luxurious, country chic aesthetic.

Sensational seafood specials are delivered with exceptional quality at The Fenwick Arms. Daily changing specials reflect the seasonality of the menu and feature the catch of the day, straight from celebrated fish monger Chris Neve at Fleetwood fishing port. The nine contemporary guest rooms are well appointed and elegant.

ADDRESS

Lancaster Road, Caton
LA2 9LA

PHONE

015242 21157

The Sausage Roll

While sausage rolls are proudly presented as a British culinary tradition, their beginnings can be found across the Channel in France some 200 years ago. The dish features puff pastry wrapped around sausage meat, which once cooked may be eaten hot or cold.

While often bite-sized, the Guinness World Records lists the longest sausage roll at a mammoth 111.11m.

The Church Inn

WA16 7RD | **CHESHIRE** | **MOBBERLEY**

Fully renovated in 2013, The Church Inn has been serving the local community since the 18th century in its rural setting 15 miles from Manchester. Under the current owners, the inn has been transformed into a tastefully different country tavern, featuring traditional tiled and timber floors, a wooden bar and stone fireplace, accented by candlelight. Join the crowd of locals in the pub, cosy up in an intimate corner or book one of two private dining rooms. There are also rustic tables on the terrace with a charming church view.

As much of the menu as possible is created from locally sourced ingredients and artisan suppliers. The pub also proudly purveys a selection of ales brewed within 15 miles of Mobberley.

ADDRESS
Church Lane, Mobberley
WA16 7RD

PHONE
01565 873178

The Vicarage Freehouse

CW4 8EF | CHESHIRE | CRANAGE

Grade II-listed elegance in the Cheshire countryside, The Vicarage Freehouse is a luxurious bolthole 30 miles south of Manchester and approximately 20 miles east of the Peak District National Park. The pub offers a stylishly historic setting to drink and dine – sink into the sofas surrounding the fireplace, pull up an antique chair or bag a spot at the bar.

Breakfast, lunch, dinner and afternoon tea are all served at The Vicarage, which has built a reputation for its beautifully presented dishes. Many of the ingredients are supplied by growers and producers in the local area. Combined with 26 country-luxe bedrooms, there are plenty of reasons to make a weekend of it here.

ADDRESS
Knutsford Road, Cranage
CW4 8EF

PHONE
01477 533393

The Wateredge Inn

LA22 0EP | **CUMBRIA** | AMBLESIDE

Perched on the glistening shore of Lake Windermere, The Wateredge Inn promises one of the best views in the Lake District. With its own jetty and a beer garden that looks straight out over the water to the hills beyond, you'll struggle to find a better place for a pint with a view. And with local real ales on tap, you really can drink in the product of those views.

The inn dates back to the 17th century and combines modern comforts with character features, so you can relax into contemporary leather chairs while centuries-old beams hang overhead or escape to one of the luxuriously decorated bedrooms. You'll find the menu proudly championing Cumbrian food, with plenty to fill your boots after a day on the fells.

ADDRESS
Borrans Rd, Ambleside
LA22 0EP

PHONE
015394 32332

The Pheasant

CH3 9PF | **CHESHIRE** | CHESTER

The Pheasant enjoys one of the most impressive views in Cheshire, with uninterrupted vistas over lush countryside stretching all the way to Wales. This cosy, traditional, sandstone pub has occupied its prime position for close to 400 years and, thanks to sympathetic renovations, it's now an atmospheric, warm and welcoming destination, packed to the rafters with character features.

The menu leans towards fresh and seasonal ingredients and offers visitors the chance to taste a whole host of local flavours, including five different Cheshire cheeses. A commitment that has earned the inn AA Rosette acclaim. Character bedrooms are available in the inn and converted stables with walking, cycling and fishing to enjoy close by.

ADDRESS

Pennsylvania Lane, Higher Burwardsley
CH3 9PF

PHONE

01829 770434

"You meet a better class of
person in pubs"

Oliver Reed

The Fat Lamb

CA17 4LL | CUMBRIA | KIRKBY STEPHEN

The Fat Lamb is a traditional stone inn situated in the untamed Yorkshire Dales National Park. Serving both the local community of Kirkby Stephen and the many walkers who come to explore the North's wildest corners, the home-cooked dishes are hearty and filling – just what you need after a day on the hills or in the nearby Lake District.

The inn lies on a crossroads, giving an authentic taste of the coaching inns that punctuated journeys in times past. You can still stay at The Fat Lamb today. There are 12 comfortable bedrooms that have been awarded four stars by the AA.

ADDRESS

Crossbank, Ravenstonedale, Kirkby Stephen
CA17 4LL

PHONE

015396 23242

Kirkby Lonsdale Brewery

LA6 2AB | **CUMBRIA** | KIRKBY LONSDALE

Contemporary, charming and cool – Kirkby Lonsdale Brewery may only have opened in 2009, but it's fast built a reputation for brilliantly brewed beers in a uniquely rustic, stylish setting. Now brewing 36 barrels a week, it's firmly on the map.

Pay the brewery a visit and sip real ales named after the local area in the tap house, otherwise known as the Royal Barn. A vaulted ceiling, huge beams and reclaimed timber furnishings give this space a serious sense of cool, making it a booze destination for every generation. There's a cosy wood burning stove to congregate around and an undeniable buzz when the room fills up.

ADDRESS
New Road, Kirkby Lonsdale
LA6 2AB

PHONE
015242 72221

The Punch Bowl

LA8 8HR | **CUMBRIA** | CROSTHWAITE

The Punch Bowl is a historic stone inn set in Cumbria's picturesque Lyth Valley, a quiet corner of the Lake District with rolling, rural views. It's ideal for a luxurious country retreat, with an elegant beamed dining room lit by candles and nine charming bedrooms featuring roll-top bathtubs. Each room offers a snapshot of local history, being named after vicars of the neighbouring church.

The bar is a homely collection of antique furniture and restored features, like the slate floor. A stone fireplace creates a feature in the dining room – an intimate space in which to sample the unfussy but expertly prepared menu that fuses the best of British and French cuisine.

ADDRESS
Crosthwaite Lyth Valley, Kendal
LA8 8HR

PHONE
015395 68237

The Factory Tap

LA9 7DE | CUMBRIA | KENDAL

The Factory Tap is the Lake District's hippest real ale venue. Within its character stone walls, a cornucopia of craft beers awaits, which have been lovingly selected by landlord Les Brown. And while this is definitely a destination for hop-lovers, grape buffs will appreciate the range of wines on offer too. At the bar, there's an intoxicating mix of international and local ales to enjoy, many of which the team will proudly point out, are created in Cumbria's own 40 breweries.

There's a courtyard beer garden out front, which is great for watching village life rumble by and dogs are welcome too. Time your visit to coincide with The Factory Tap's monthly street food event – you won't be disappointed.

ADDRESS

5 Aynam Rd, Kendal
LA9 7DE

PHONE

01539 482541

The Aspinall Arms

BB7 9PQ | LANCASHIRE | CLITHEROE

With a beer garden that rolls down to the flowing river Ribble and a medieval church beyond, it's fair to say that the 17th century Aspinall Arms has a setting few pubs can rival. Few can rival the freshness of their menus either – no two days are the same – or the unassuming charm of the pub's country interiors.

Open fires, flagstone floors and shelves brimming with books create a welcoming, relaxed feel at The Aspinall Arms. The food promises an unfussy feast of British classics, which pair beautifully with the international selection of wines. Located midway between the Forest of Bowland and Pendle Hill, this pub is a haven for hikers.

ADDRESS
Mitton Rd, Clitheroe, Lancashire
BB7 9PQ

PHONE
01254 826555

Coniston

NORTH WEST | PLACES WE LOVE |

Coniston was historically famous for its ore and slate mining. During Victorian times, the Furness Railway terminated in Coniston which opened up tourism to this beautiful area. Today hill-walking, rock-climbing and boating are popular pursuits from the village base.

Ambleside

NORTH WEST | PLACES WE LOVE |

Ambleside has a rich Roman history, with a fort named Galava, dating from AD79 and situated just south of the town. Today it serves as a base for those exploring the surrounding countryside and is particularly popular with climbers, hikers and mountain bikers.

Grasmere

NORTH WEST | PLACES WE LOVE |

Situated in the centre of the Lake District, Grasmere is best known for its famous resident, the poet William Wordsworth who described it as "the loveliest spot that man hath ever found." Its enchanting beauty attracts visitors from all over the world. Today the town is a tourist destination and offers a wide range of gift shops, cafés and accommodation.

Cartmel

NORTH WEST | PLACES WE LOVE |

The South Lakeland District fells and countryside surround Cartmel and its famous 12th Century medieval Priory Church offers centuries of enthralling history. The village itself offers great food and dining opportunities from artisan bread and cheese shops to traditional pubs.

Kirkby Lonsdale

NORTH WEST | PLACES WE LOVE |

Kirkby Lonsdale is situated on the river Lune and on the edge of the Yorkshire Dales. Popular with walkers and cyclists, the Three Peaks are close by, making it an appealing base for those touring the area. This scenic small town is full of stone-built houses and plenty of respected restaurants, pubs and hotels.

St. Bees

NORTH WEST | PLACES WE LOVE |

St. Bees is well-known for its Norman Priory dating from 1120 and for being the starting point of the Wainwright "Coast to Coast" Walk. Just 50 miles south of the Scottish border, this coastal town has a large sandy beach and has been a popular tourist destination for 150 years.

Buttermere

NORTH WEST | PLACES WE LOVE |

Buttermere is surrounded by vertiginous mountains and tranquil countryside. The path that runs the perimeter of Buttermere Lake can be completed within two to three hours and is popular with families. Owned by The National Trust, Buttermere Lake is renowned for its natural beauty and its name means 'lake by the dairy pastures'.

Bowness-on-Windermere

NORTH WEST | PLACES WE LOVE |

Situated on the shore of Lake Windermere, Bowness-on-Windermere is one of the most popular tourist destinations in the Lake District due to it being a centre for outdoor and adventure activities. From a humble fishing village to a vibrant tourist destination, a number of the hotels today have been converted from large Victorian residences.

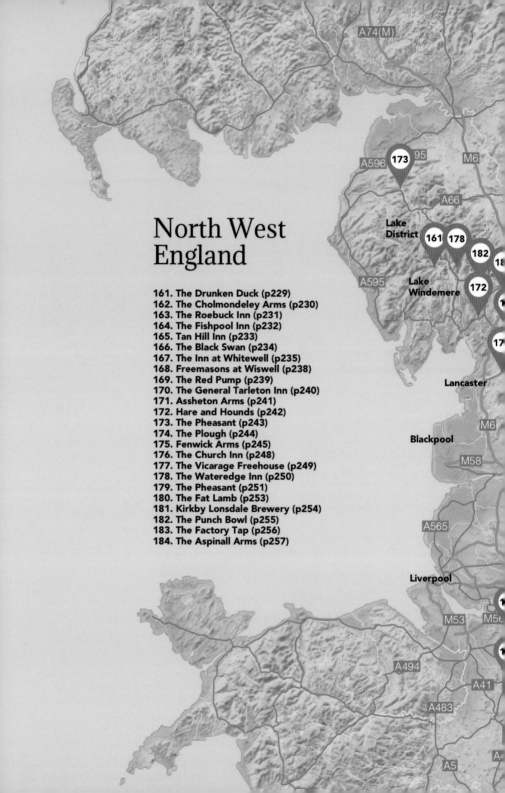

North West England

CHAPTER SEVEN

NORTH
EAST

The Star Inn

YO62 5JE | YORKSHIRE | HELMSLEY

Some six hundred years have made The Star Inn the charming pub that it is today. And what a pub, with food inspired by the inn's North York Moors location that has earned it a prestigious Michelin star. A title they have proudly held for four years in a row now.

With stained glass, timber and bags of country appeal, The Star is a real treat whether you want to refuel after a hike or enjoy a celebratory meal. Next door, the inn also offers a boutique-style hotel – you'll need to stay nine times to discover each bedroom's unique quirks, but just one visit to The Wheelhouse for breakfast will bowl you over.

ADDRESS

Main Street, Harome, Helmsley
YO62 5JE

PHONE

01439 770397

The Lister Arms

BD23 4DB | YORKSHIRE | MALHAM

The Lister Arms in Malham is a traditional coaching inn with captivating period features and an exterior embellished in vibrant green foliage. The inn's interior has been modernised whilst retaining its rich history and features, from its beams and wooden floors to its original fireplaces.

Local, seasonal ingredients from trusted suppliers are the focus of the traditional menu at The Lister Arms in Malham. Particularly popular with walkers, due to its idyllic position within the Yorkshire Dales, the inviting ambience and roaring log fires make this a great spot to stop for food or a drink.

ADDRESS

Skipton, Malham
BD23 4DB

PHONE

01729 830330

Craven Arms

BD23 6DA | YORKSHIRE | APPLETREEWICK

The Craven Arms in Appletreewick is a picture-postcard, old English pub, with a great reputation for its food and real ale. The ale is all traditionally cask-conditioned and the artisan dishes are lovingly prepared from local ingredients on the premises.

The Craven Arms began its life as a 16th-century farmhouse and many of its original features remain. Open fires create a cosy atmosphere and on warmer days, you can enjoy views of the spectacular scenery from the garden. The pub has its own herb garden and the thatched Cruck Barn hosts many events and functions.

ADDRESS

Skipton, Appletreewick
BD23 6DA

PHONE

01756 720270

Cook & Barker

NE65 9JY | NORTHUMBERLAND | MORPETH

A postcard of rural England, Newton-on-the-Moor's Cook & Barker Inn welcomes patrons with a charming stone façade, overflowing with flowers and country appeal. It's a rustic style that continues inside, with a distinctly luxurious touch. Think button-back seats, timber floorboards and exposed brick walls.

In the restaurant, the menu is inspired by the pub's location close to both the coast and the Cheviot Hills, featuring seafood, grills and traditional classics, each creatively plated. Upstairs, the 14 en-suite bedrooms and two suites invite visitors to make a weekend of it, dozing in roomy beds beneath characterful beamed ceilings.

ADDRESS

Newton-on-the-Moor, Morpeth
NE65 9JY

PHONE

01665 575234

The Kings Head

BD23 5RD | YORKSHIRE | KETTLEWELL

The Kings Head at Kettlewell is an exceptional and award-winning pub with national recognition for its food and accommodation. Surrounded by some of Yorkshire's most scenic countryside, The Kings Head's menu specialises in a modern approach to traditional British pub classics.

People come from far and wide to taste the delicious and traditional yet refined dishes at The Kings Head. The pub's interior is light and contemporary with original character features including the fireplaces and stone flooring, which complement the soft neutral and ambient colour scheme. There are five en-suite guest rooms.

ADDRESS

The Green, Kettlewell
BD23 5RD

PHONE

01756 761600

Lorde Crewe Arms

DH8 9SP | NORTHUMBERLAND | BLANCHLAND

A quintessential country retreat, one visit to the Lorde Crewe Arms and you will never wish to leave. The golden stone inn sits at the heart of sleepy, manicured Blanchland – a surreal contrast to the untamed beauty of the North Pennine Moors that cocoon it. Explore the wild Northumbrian surroundings and stay the night in one of the inn's quietly charming rooms.

Headed up by chef Simon Hicks, the pub pedals hearty, local, home-grown fare that is guaranteed to surprise you. But an even greater surprise awaits at the bar, otherwise known as The Crypt. Drinking here means quaffing local ales, including the inn's eponymous Lord Crewe Brew, in what feels like a cellar, with exposed stone walls that curve up and over you.

ADDRESS

The Square, Blanchland DH8 9SP

DH8 9SP

PHONE

01434 677100

The Fountaine Inn

BD23 5HJ | **YORKSHIRE** | **LINTON IN CRAVEN**

The Fountaine Inn is a pub with personality. Situated in the stunning Yorkshire countryside, this inn is about community and great hospitality. Its stylish interior fuses modern with traditional, with a fun mix of textures, colours and patterns to create a vibrant atmosphere.

From imaginative recipes to simple pub classics, the menu at The Fountaine Inn sources local ingredients from suppliers in the region. The open fires create a cosy environment and guest rooms with a similar contemporary style within the pub's traditional surroundings are also available.

ADDRESS

Linton in Craven
BD23 5HJ

PHONE

01756 752210

The Scotch Egg

Another classic English treat, the Scotch egg is the perfect picnic accompaniment with high beginnings, as Fortnum & Mason claim to have made the first. The pinnacle of success on the gastro scene is the ability to retain an oozing yolk.

Traditionally created with a boiled hen's egg, sausage meat and a bread crumb shell, quail and duck eggs are also popular.

The Star Inn

YO1 7DR | YORKSHIRE | YORK

Perched on the banks of the river Ouse in the medieval city of York, The Star Inn isn't afraid to make a splash. Inside the former Engine House, a dramatic double-height space awaits that is eclectic and atmospheric in equal measure. The feel is warm, inviting and quirky. But don't be fooled into thinking the copper beer tanks define the bar menu – with 26 gins alone, there's plenty of choice.

On a summer's day, enjoy drinks and dinner outside on the terrace to make the most of The Star Inn's waterside location. Whether you visit for breakfast, lunch or dinner, expect a menu that is propelled by the seasons and that places provenance of ingredients at its heart.

ADDRESS

Lendal Engine House, Museum Street, York
YO1 7DR

PHONE

01904 619208

The Goodmanham Arms

YO43 3JA | YORKSHIRE | YORK

The Goodmanham Arms is a cosy, red brick pub located 45 minutes from York in the village from which it takes its name. It's an alehouse that feels at once as if tradition is bound into the building, while still welcoming customs new. The micro-brewery across the road is a testament to this.

Guided by owners of the pub, Vito and Abbie Loggozi, the old brewery has taken on a new lease of life and now creates the Peg Fyfe, Mischief Maker and Ragged Robyn real ales that you'll find stocked behind The Goodmanham Arms' bar. Those who prefer to combine liquid and edible indulgence will find the pub's honest, traditional menu a welcome addition, to be enjoyed in a cosy corner of this proudly rustic pub.

ADDRESS

Main Street, Goodmanham,
York
YO43 3JA

PHONE

01430 873849

The Feathers Inn

NE43 7SW | NORTHUMBERLAND | STOCKSFIELD

The traditional stone exterior of The Feathers Inn in Hedley on the Hill packs plenty of appeal, but it's the award-winning menu that draws patrons from far and wide. Owners Rhian and Helen have steered the Northumbrian inn to success and now, in addition to hosting a lively crowd of locals, the pub is also the hub for events and a cookery school.

Located 15 minutes from Newcastle to the east of the North Pennines, the menu is a celebration of all things locally grown, reared and produced and openly so, naming the farms and suppliers with the ingredient. Such a commitment to seasonal, regional dining isn't without effort – the menu changes twice each day, keeping the chefs busy and visitors delighted with the variety.

ADDRESS

High View, Hedley on the Hill,
Stocksfield
NE43 7SW

PHONE

01661 843607

The Duke of Wellington Inn

NE43 7UL | NORTHUMBERLAND | STOCKSFIELD

Located a short journey from Hadrian's Wall, The Duke of Wellington Inn has undergone a sympathetic restoration and now offers an atmospheric restaurant and seven uniquely styled bedrooms. Thanks to the pub's elevated position, you can enjoy sweeping, bucolic views over rolling hills whether you're sipping a pint, tucking into AA-rosette cuisine or dozing off.

The bar is blissfully traditional, with darts, cards and a fire the perfect accompaniments to the line-up of cask ales, keg beers and spirits. With exposed stone walls, the restaurant retains the rural charm but with a more refined finish, perfectly complemented by chef Dave Mckie's fine dining menu.

ADDRESS

Newton, Stocksfield
NE43 7UL

PHONE

01661 844446

PLACES WE LOVE

Seven Sisters, Sussex

Barrasford Arms

NE48 4AA | NORTHUMBERLAND | HEXHAM

Hexham's Barrasford Arms ramps up the style stakes, offering a welcoming country inn with a distinctly modern, refined flair. A feature fireplace and large sash windows ground the dining room in a sense of history, while also making the most of the pub's idyllic Northumbrian countryside views.

Championing local suppliers and working with the seasons, The Barrasford Arms dates back to the 1800's. Overlooking Houghton Castle, this picturesque pub uses ingredients from its own polytunnel and gardens. It also happens to be perfectly positioned for those exploring Hadrian's Wall.

ADDRESS

Barrasford, Hexham
NE48 4AA

PHONE

01434 681237

The Joiners Arms

NE66 3EA | **NORTHUMBERLAND** | ALNWICK

Located just a stone's throw from the water in Newton-by-the-Sea, The Joiners Arms promises a sense of theatre few inns can rival. From the moody, timber-clad bar to the gastro menu and dramatically decorated bedrooms, every moment here is an experience.

Committed to cooking local ingredients for villagers and visitors alike to enjoy, the menu offers a hearty range from the catch-of-the-day to seasonal specials and sizzling steaks. Dogs are as welcome as their owners at The Joiners Arms, making it the perfect spot to stop after a bracing coastal walk or visit to Alnwick Castle.

ADDRESS
Newton-by-the-Sea, Alnwick
NE66 3EA

PHONE
01665 576 112

The Jolly Fisherman

NE66 3TR | **NORTHUMBERLAND** | **CRASTER**

First opened in 1847, The Jolly Fisherman has been serving the local community of Craster for over 150 years from its seafront perch. It only makes sense then, that the menu majors on freshly caught fish and seafood, headed up by high-flying chef Kevin Mulraney. Ingredients are locally sourced with their provenance often traced so that you can follow the journey from producer to plate.

The inn has a seafaring charm to its refurbished interiors, pairing timber-clad walls with exposed stone and cosy soft furnishings, all atmospherically lit by ship lanterns. The bustling bar changes like the tides, welcoming guest ales to its ranks alongside its stalwart cask beers – Workie Ticket and Black Sheep.

ADDRESS

9 Haven Hill, Craster
NE66 3RT

PHONE

01665 576 461

The Ship Inn

NE66 3EL | NORTHUMBERLAND | ALNWICK

The Ship Inn's present-day incarnation stemmed from a spontaneous decision made by owner Christine Forsyth almost 20 years ago. In the time since, the pub has been lovingly renovated in an unassuming, country style – think exposed stone walls, hops hanging from the ceiling and a cosy log burning stove. It has also welcomed a micro-brewery, which for the last 10 years has kept the bar flowing with real ales – over 26 in fact.

Making the most of their seaside location in Low Newton, The Ship Inn celebrates local ingredients and flavours on its home-cooked menu, including lobster from the bay in season. Live music is often on the agenda, offering dinner and drinks with a buzz.

ADDRESS

Low Newton-by-the-Sea,
Alnwick
NE66 3EL

PHONE

01665 576262

The Pheasant

NE48 1DD | **NORTHUMBERLAND** | HEXHAM

A 400-year-old former farmhouse only a mile from Kielder Water, The Pheasant Inn has oodles of country appeal. Its honey-stone exterior is covered in rambling climbers, while the pub inside has a cosy atmosphere with dark beams, stone fireplaces and character tartans.

In the kitchen, the focus is firmly on fresh and local ingredients, some of which are harvested from the pub's well-tended fruit and vegetable garden. The taste of Northern England evolves behind the bar, where you'll find Wylam Brewery ales among the local selection, as well as 50 malt whiskies. With character, personality and eight en-suite bedrooms upstairs, it's easy to imagine staying a while...

ADDRESS
Shilling Pot, Stannersburn,
Hexham
NE48 1DD

PHONE
01434 240382

"There is nothing which has yet been contrived by man, by which so much happiness is produced as by a good tavern"

Samuel Johnson

Whitby

NORTH EAST | PLACES WE LOVE |

Situated at the mouth of the river Esk on Yorkshire's East coast, Whitby is a traditional seaside resort and port with an interesting history and scenic views. With an active local fishing industry making use of the port, restaurants specialising in seafood and fish and chips are nationally renowned.

Saltburn-by-the-Sea

NORTH EAST | PLACES WE LOVE |

Saltburn by the Sea is a laid back Victorian seaside town renowned for its slow pace and surfing. Its Victorian pier has survived almost 150 years of extreme weather, as England's most northerly pier and the town itself is proud of its smuggling past and celebrated Victorian constructions, from its railway to its cliff lift.

York

NORTH EAST | PLACES WE LOVE |

York is a picturesque, riverside city brimming with fascinating history and cosmopolitan charm. Its famous walls, impressive architecture and cobbled streets create an awe-inspiring backdrop to this popular city. The striking stained glass windows in the Gothic Cathedral captivate visitors with their resplendent vibrancy.

Harrogate

NORTH EAST | PLACES WE LOVE |

The elegant, Victorian spa town of Harrogate was famous for its healing, mineral spring water. During the 17th and 18th centuries, Harrogate became a spa town destination. Today the town celebrates its history and offers abundant floral gardens, a respected theatre and quality, independent boutiques.

Skipton

NORTH EAST | PLACES WE LOVE |

The scenic, market town of Skipton is situated in the foothills of the Dales and has won numerous awards for its popular high street and the happiness of its inhabitants. Its spellbinding, medieval castle is over 900 years old and beautifully preserved and maintained.

Goathland

NORTH EAST | PLACES WE LOVE |

Goathland is a refreshing moorland village in the center of the North York National Park. The village has become increasingly popular as a tourist destination due to its role as Aidensfield in the TV series Heartbeat. Lots of old cars and business names are the same as in the series and a delight for Heartbeat enthusiasts.

Thornton le Dale

NORTH EAST | PLACES WE LOVE |

Thornton le Dale has won countless awards for being Britain's most attractive town, with its thatched cottages, gentle stream running alongside the Main Street and pretty gardens. The village is certainly picturesque and highly photographed; you might have seen the thatched cottage by the 'babbling beck' on a number of chocolate boxes and sweet selections.

Beverley

NORTH EAST | PLACES WE LOVE |

Beverley in East Yorkshire is a peaceful market town known primarily for its Medieval history and its imposing 13th century Minster, one of Europe's finest surviving Gothic churches. Today Beverley hosts many food and music festivals and celebrated horse races on its famous track.

Scarborough

NORTH EAST | PLACES WE LOVE |

Scarborough has been a go-to holiday destination in the UK for almost 400 years. Two bays with glorious golden sand offer a great day out for all the family. The South Bay is filled with sparkly amusement arcades and spade shops, whereas the North Bay is much quieter with rows of colourful beach huts and a waterpark.

Ripon

NORTH EAST | PLACES WE LOVE |

The city of Ripon, founded 1300 years ago, is located in North Yorkshire on the River Ure. This pretty market town is celebrated as a Cathedral City, where monasteries have stood since the 7th Century. With a popular market and a famous horse-racing track, Ripon also offers an abundance of boutiques, restaurants and cafes.

Robin Hood's Bay

NORTH EAST | PLACES WE LOVE |

Robin Hood's Bay is a rustic coastal area in Yorkshire, loved for its rugged and inspiring beauty. Old fisherman cottages and ancient inns are sprinkled around this scenic bay, which attracts walkers, horse riders and those that enjoy the water. There are also good cafes and restaurants specialising in seafood and cream teas in this area.

Alnmouth

NORTH EAST | PLACES WE LOVE |

Alnmouth is a beautiful historic village, based along the stunning Northumberland coast. Highlights include the vast clean sandy beaches that stretch for miles and the colourful houses that run along the bank of the River Aln. A great spot for refreshment is Scotts of Alnmouth, where you can pick up some decent grub and artisan coffee.

Craster

Craster is a small fishing village on the Northumberland coast. There is a small harbour with a handful of boats and a short stroll north brings you to the ruins of Dunstanburgh Castle. Craster is famous for it's smoked kippers, so pop into the smokehouse where they have been curing fish for the past 130 years.

Helmsley

NORTH EAST | PLACES WE LOVE |

Helmsley is the only market town in the North York Moors National Park and has plenty of attractions to lure visitors. Both Helmsley Castle and the Walled Garden are ideal ways to spend half days immersed in history and you are spoilt for choice when it comes to places to eat.

Bamburgh

NORTH EAST | PLACES WE LOVE |

Bamburgh is a quaint coastal village in the heart of Northumberland. Thousands flock to Bamburgh each year to see its epic castle which dominates the skyline. Either side of the Castle are endless clean sandy beaches and interesting rock formations, ideal for walking and family holidays on the sand.

Yorkshire Dales

NORTH EAST | PLACES WE LOVE |

The Yorkshire Dales stands out as one of England's more dramatically scenic places to visit. It's renowned for its brilliant walking territory, wild landscapes, waterfalls and drystone walls. Stone-built villages split up the meandering roads and scattered remains of former working mines. Highlights include Skipton, Richmond, Hawes, Kirkby Stephen and Sedburgh.

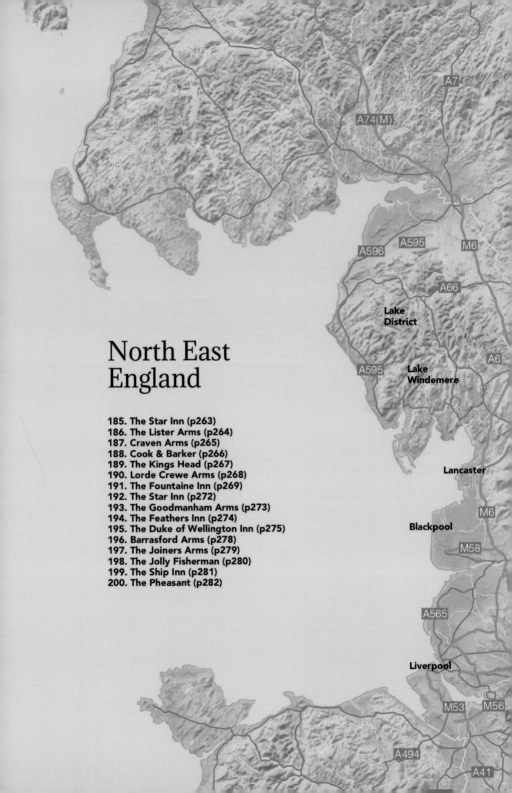

North East England

Meet the family

A series of 8 unique travel guides.

Every guide contains a curated selection of recommendations, each one hand picked and photographed by the Best of England team.

None of the businesses have paid to be included so our guides are 100% honest and based on our own experiences.